Calligraphy
step-by-step

Calligraphy

step-by-step

A structured course in fine writing

GAYNOR GOFFE & ANNA RAVENSCROFT

BCA

LONDON   NEW YORK   SYDNEY   TORONTO

This edition published 1994
by BCA by arrangement with
HarperCollins Publishers

CN 9446

First published in 1994 by
HarperCollins Publishers, London

A catalogue record for this book is available from the
British Library

This book was designed and produced by
Quarto Publishing plc
The Old Brewery
6 Blundell Street
London N7 9BH

Senior Editor *Cathy Meeus*
Senior Art Editor *Penny Cobb*
Designer *Hugh Schermuly*
Picture Manager *Giulia Hetherington*
Photographers *Paul Forrester, Chas Wilder*
Illustrators *David Kemp, Ed Stuart*
Editorial Director *Sophie Collins*
Art Director *Moira Clinch*

All calligraphic examples are by the authors except
where otherwise stated in the credits on page 176.

The credits that appear on page 176 are hereby made a
part of this copyright page.

Typeset in Great Britain by En-to-En, Tunbridge Wells
Manufactured in Singapore by Eray Scan Pte Ltd.
Printed in Singapore by Star Standard Industries (Pte) Ltd.

Foreword

There are so many exciting possibilities in calligraphy — from elegant invitations to personalized greetings cards — that it is tempting to try everything. However, once you become familiar with calligraphic principles, you soon realize that the skills need to be learned one step at a time.

Written specifically for the beginner, this step-by-step guide is designed to enable the reader to acquire a useful range of working skills in a logical sequence. Throughout the book, practical exercises allow the beginner progressively to build a sound body of knowledge, from alphabets to using colour.

You do not need a vast store of expensive materials and equipment to learn calligraphy. The first lessons in this book require little more than paper, pencil and a ruler. Part 2 introduces the use of the edged (or broad-nibbed) pen. Essential confidence-building

techniques for handling the pen are explained, as well as the fundamental principles underlying all calligraphic scripts. The basics of arranging your lettering pleasingly on the page are also discussed in detail.

The main scripts used by calligraphers today are described in Part 3. Mastery of these letterforms will equip you for an interesting range of calligraphy projects and annotated calligraphic examples and helpful checklists will encourage you to develop a critical eye and to learn from your mistakes. However, calligraphy is about more than just letterforms. Effective interpretation of a text is enhanced by the use of colour and illustration, and in Part 4 you will find plenty of information on how to make your work more decorative.

The final section of this book, the project section, shows some of the uses to which you can put your calligraphy. Each project follows the development of a piece of calligraphic work step by step from initial idea to finished item. Designed to be within easy reach of the calligraphy beginner, these projects will help you to consolidate the skills you have learned and put them to practical use.

Calligraphy is a demanding but immensely satisfying craft that offers endless creativity.

Gaynor Goffe and Anna Ravenscroft

Contents

MASTERING THE LETTERFORMS

COLOUR AND IMAGE

PROJECTS

Calligraphy

In Britain and the United States, as well as parts of Europe, recent decades have witnessed a widespread revival of interest in all aspects of calligraphy — in graphic design as a craft and as an artistic medium for self-expression. Calligraphy is now viewed as a tradition with contemporary relevance, rather than an outmoded and archaic practice.

Today's calligraphers have a superb heritage of over 2,000 years of development of the Roman alphabet on which they can draw for their scripts. However experimental you may wish your calligraphy to be, the use of these historical scripts as a basis for your work is vitally important. Such precedents are the roots of modern calligraphy, and have a vast wealth of inspiration to offer to every contemporary calligrapher.

THE BEGINNINGS OF CALLIGRAPHY

The earliest examples of the Roman alphabet we use today date from the third century B.C. These early Roman capitals were mostly found incised into stone. Although, later, there were pen-written Roman capitals, the inscriptional forms — in particular those on Trajan's Column (c. A.D. 114) in Rome — remain unsurpassed as a historical reference.

Other pen-made scripts in use in Roman times include Roman square capitals (quadrata), Rustica (there are also brush-made forms of this script in existence), and Roman cursive — a flowing, everyday script which was

ROMAN CAPITALS

These incised letters from the Roman Forum (below) are examples of the letterforms from which modern pen-made Roman capitals are derived.

I WENT TO THE WOODS BECAUSE
I WISHED TO LIVE DELIBERATELY
TO FRONT ONLY THE ESSENTIAL FACTS OF LIFE
& SEE IF I COULD NOT LEARN
WHAT IT HAD TO TEACH
AND NOT, WHEN I CAME TO DIE
DISCOVER THAT I HAD NOT LIVED

Thoreau

inscribed into clay and lead tablets and also written on papyrus. This last script was the first in which we see ascenders and descenders.

After the decline of the Roman Empire, the main scripts to be developed were uncials and half uncials, both influenced by Roman precedents. The half uncials found in the English Lindisfarne Gospels and the Irish Book of Kells mark the highpoint of fine writing during the Dark Ages in Europe.

The court of the Emperor Charlemagne was the source of the next major development in scripts. In 789, Charlemagne, seeking to standardize the great variety of scripts in use throughout his domains, decreed that the round bookhand that we now know as Carolingian minuscule be used. The capitals most often used with this script were pen-made, built-up versions of Roman capitals — versals. They were often highly decorated.

I WENT TO THE WOODS
John Nash

This elegant panel of poetry by Henry David Thoreau (above), written in built-up versal-type capitals, shows the timeless craftsmanship of fine calligraphy.
Dimensions:
23 cm × 56 cm
(9″ × 22″).

BOOK OF KELLS

This supreme example of half uncials (above), with its delicate ornamentation, was written by Irish scribes in the eighth century.

ALPHABET DESIGN
Donald Jackson

This eye-catching alphabet design (left) shows a delicate tension between gilded classical Roman capitals and the freely written uncial-influenced capitals.
Dimensions:
20.5 cm × 25.5 cm
(8″ × 10″).

9

The later medieval period saw the evolution of a variety of forms of Gothic (or Black-letter) scripts, many of which are extremely complex and difficult to read.

THE INTRODUCTION OF ITALIC

The re-kindling of interest in classical learning during the Italian Renaissance, and the discovery of ancient texts, led to a revival of Roman capitals and Carolingian minuscules as a basis for formal writing. The Humanist minuscule was an evolution of the latter. The greatest writing landmark of the Renaissance was, however, the development of one of our most beautiful and useful scripts — italic. With its slanting, compressed and flowing letters, it was the joy of the writing masters and appeared in its myriad variations in the great writing manuals, including those of Arrighi, Palatino and Tagliente. Its long ascenders and descenders lent themselves to decorative flourishing, while its speed made it practical as a chancery script too.

THE LATE-19th-CENTURY REVIVAL

In the period following the Renaissance, edged-pen writing fell into decline, with the growing

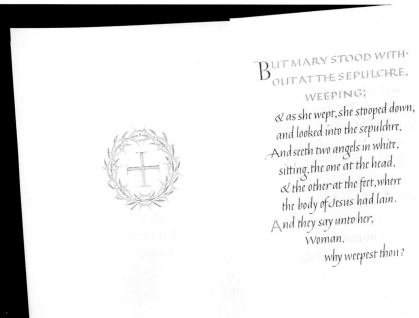

BENTIVOGLIO BOOK OF HOURS

This early-16th-century work (above) is written in a rounded Humanistic minuscule. The lavish border decoration is typical of the period.

MANUSCRIPT BOOK
Joan Pilsbury

This elegant and restrained piece of calligraphy (left) uses formal italic, a script that is a direct descendent of the letterforms used in the writing manuals of the 16th century.

COPY No. I.   *After* WINCHESTER FORMAL WRITING about 975 A.D.

Et haec scribimus vobis ut gaudeatis, & gaudium vestrum sit plenum.

Et haec est annunciatio, quam audivimus ab eo, & annunciamus vobis : Quoniam Deus lux est, & tenebrae in eo non sunt ullae.

Winchester MS. v. slightly modified

Heavy Italics based on Winchester MS.

Note: *This copy is written with a pen, not printed* Ef. 26. August 1919 A.D.

In order that a child may learn how to write well the teaching of handwriting should begin with the practice of a Formal Hand. This Manuscript is written with a BROAD-NIBBED PEN which makes the strokes thick or thin according to the direction in which it moves. The strokes are generally begun downwards or forwards & the letters are formed of several strokes *(the pen being lifted after each stroke):* abcx'l curve down, 2nd. a short thin stroke up *(the thus c consists of two strokes, the first a* nib for this stroke being placed on the beginning long curve down, the second a short curve *of the first and slid up to the right),* 3rd. the forward. The triangular 'heads' (as for *b* or *d)* thick straight *stem* stroke of the letter itself are made by *three* strokes; 1st. a short thick down *(the pen for this stroke not being lifted).*

Broad-nibbed steel pens and Reeds may be used: Quill pens are very good but require special cutting.   How to cut Quill and Reed pens may be learned from my Handbook "Writing & Illuminating, & Lettering" (*John Hogg, London:* 7s. 6d. *net*) besides how to make MS. Books and to write in colour.   Edward Johnston: *Ditchling, Sussex.*

THIS SHEET IS PUBLISHED BY DOUGLAS PEPLER at HAMPSHIRE HOUSE HAMMERSMITH 1916 A.D.

SAMPLE SHEET
Edward Johnston

Working in the early part of the 20th century, Edward Johnston produced this roundhand script based on the letterforms of the 10th century Ramsey Psalter (see p. 54).

ascendency of pointed-pen copperplate writing. It was not until the late 19th century that the practice of edged-pen calligraphy was revived by William Morris, the key figure in the Arts and Crafts Movement. He owned and was influenced by Renaissance manuscripts, and, through his own manuscript books, he engendered an appreciation of the potential of calligraphy in a contemporary setting.

The calligraphic revival was taken further by Edward Johnston, whose pioneering work in the early part of this century involving the

study of historical manuscripts resulted in a formal analysis of the letterforms and the principles of edged-pen calligraphy.

In the United States, the revival of edged-pen skills was led in the early part of this century by Ernst Detterer, who had studied with Johnston and, independently, John Howard Benson, a Rhode Island stone cutter, and Graham Casey, who, inspired by Johnston's manual, wrote *Elements of Lettering*.

CALLIGRAPHY IN THE MODERN WORLD

From the middle of this century onwards, many fine calligraphers have emerged on both sides of the Atlantic. The increasing use of calligraphy in graphic design has provided an additional impetus. The craft is now witnessing a popularity unprecedented in terms of the number of practitioners, not only in Britain and the United States, but also in Australia and throughout Europe. The great variety of cultural traditions in which today's calligraphers work has given contemporary calligraphic work a wonderful breadth and vigour.

Not only does calligraphy have commercial potential, particularly in graphic design, but it is also growing in popularity as an expressive art form, and continuing to hold an ever-increasing following as a fine craft. Calligraphy is a skill that is open to all. Whether you have had formal art training or not, there are unlimited possibilities for development along individual paths. Calligraphy brings much creative satisfaction, whatever your level of interest and expertise.

POEM
Magnus Aström

This dramatic image (above), inspired by a poem by Yvan Goll, shows a successful fusing of illustration and text in a modern context. Dimensions: 61 cm × 38 cm (24″ × 15″).

THE SHIELD OF ACHILLES
Florian Kynman

An unusual and exciting rendering of a poem by W. H. Auden. Dimensions: 61 cm × 95 cm (17½″ × 24″).

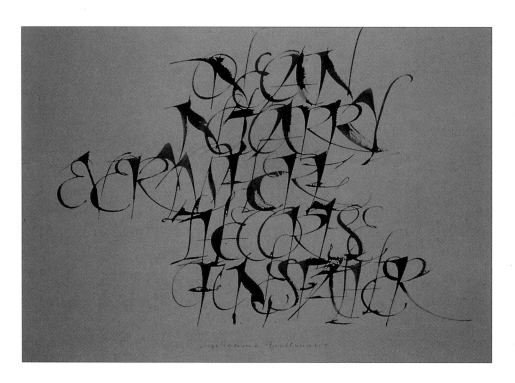

SPRING'S FIREBIRD
Ewan Clayton

In this panel (above) the Roman capitals illustrate how a traditional letterform can be taken in a contemporary direction. Dimensions: 51 cm × 76 cm (20" × 30").

TEXT BY APOLLINAIRE
Julia Vance

The delicate and striking texture of these capitals (left), punctuated by subtle use of colour, has a powerful presence. Dimensions: 46 cm × 56 cm (18" × 22").

13

1

Laying the foundations

Getting started

The materials for starting calligraphy are simple, inexpensive and easy to obtain. Pencils, paper, a ruler and a simple board are all the basic equipment you need. Add to these a few of the items listed opposite. Choosing the right tools at the start, and providing yourself with a suitable work surface and comfortable writing position, will speed the development of your skills.

Pencils for writing and for ruling lines should be relatively hard: HB or B will give lines that are sharp but easily erased. The points should be fine but not so sharp that they break easily. It helps to begin sharpening with a pencil sharpener or knife and to finish with fine sandpaper. You will also need a clean soft eraser for correcting mistakes. For ruling lines, choose a sturdy metal or metal-edged ruler — plastic may chip or warp. In addition, you should obtain a large set square (with sides about 30 cm [12″] in length).

Newsprint is an inexpensive choice for pencil practice, or you can use drawing paper — in sheets or a pad. Layout paper, available as single sheets or in pads from art-materials shops, is useful for planning and doing creative work. Avoid paper with shiny, textured or overly rough surfaces, as these may affect the flow of your writing.

A board is essential to provide a firm writing surface of adequate size. If the board is too small, it will restrict your arm movement and hamper your writing. Do not be lured at this stage by some of the sophisticated table easels and adjustable boards to be found on the market. Many professional calligraphers produce work of the finest quality without such equipment. Buy a simple board, or make your own (see facing page). This may save money and will ensure the correct size.

PAPER
Inexpensive drawing paper or layout paper is fine for practice. Use good-quality drawing paper for finished work.

SHARPENERS
Pencils must be kept sharp. A pencil sharpener will do the job, as will a craft knife (also useful for cut-and-paste work).

PENCILS
Regular HB or slightly softer, blacker B pencils are widely available.

SANDPAPER
Finish sharpening your pencils with fine sandpaper. Either staple this around a piece of wood, or buy a ready-made sandpaper block from an art-materials shop.

BLOTTING PAPER
Soft blotting paper cushions the board and makes a good writing surface.

ERASER
It is important to find a soft, good-quality eraser.

MASKING TAPE
Masking tape is used to hold a guard sheet in position and to tape blotting paper to the board. It is also useful for holding reference material in position.

RULER AND SET SQUARE
Use a metal ruler. Its edge is less likely to get damaged. A clear plastic set square allows you to see what is underneath it while you are squaring up.

T-SQUARE AND BOARD
You will need a T-square, used in conjunction with your board and a set square, for ruling. The board should be at least 75 cm × 60 cm (30″ × 24″) and approximately 1 cm (³⁄₈″) thick.

- ✓ Pencils (HB or B)
- ✓ Drawing paper, inexpensive paper and/or layout paper
- ✓ Metal ruler
- ✓ Set square
- ✓ Soft eraser
- ✓ Pencil sharpener
- ✓ Craft knife
- ✓ Fine sandpaper or sandpaper block
- ✓ Blotting paper (to place between board and writing paper)
- ✓ Masking tape (low-tack)
- ✓ Board
- ✓ T-square

Although the way in which different calligraphers sit and hold their pens will vary slightly from person to person — just as calligraphy itself does — when beginning calligraphy it is important to give yourself the best chance of getting off to a good start by sitting correctly and using the recommended pen hold.

Writing position

The way you sit will be directly reflected in your writing. If your body is tense and angled, your hand and arm will be restricted and your writing will not flow. A poor writing position produces awkward and inconsistent letterforms, and this can be very disheartening. You need a posture that optimizes controlled but fluid movement. This means considering the position of your body and the angle of your board (see right).

Writing on an angled board gives you a good overall view of your work as it progresses and will moderate the flow of ink when you come to write with the pen. A raised board also discourages you from leaning over your work. For most writing, the board needs to be raised at an angle of 30–45°; find a position that suits you within these guidelines.

Use a table and a chair whose relative heights enable you to keep your board at the chosen angle. A table that is too low or a chair that is too high will place you in an uncomfortably high position and will in effect flatten the angle of the board.

CORRECT POSITION
The height of your table and chair should be adjusted to allow you to work with both feet placed side by side on the floor. This will ensure steadiness and reduce tension. By angling your board, you can work without leaning forward.

CROSSED LEGS

The crossed legs and twisted body angle of the person pictured would make it difficult to achieve good writing. This may seem extreme, but it is not unusual to see people assuming this posture unconsciously.

LEANING TOO FAR FORWARD

Avoid the temptation to lean forward, which will inhibit arm movement.

HOLDING THE PENCIL

Most calligraphers, whether right- or left-handed, rest the pencil lightly on the first joint of the middle finger and use the thumb and forefinger to guide the pencil point and maintain the required angle to the paper — a steeper one than that usually used for sketching.

The type and direction of the light by which you work will affect the quality of your calligraphy. The aim is to have good lighting without shadows being cast over your work. Take note of the following guidelines:

✔ Good daylight is preferable.
✔ Artificial light is best provided by an adjustable desk lamp.
✔ "Daylight" bulbs give the best artificial light, especially for work in colour.
✔ Position your light source to avoid creating shadows on your work. Light should come from your left if you are right-handed and from your right if you are left-handed.

Right-hander — light from left, no shadows on work.

Right-hander — light from right, shadows on work.

RAISING YOUR BOARD

Prop your board at the recommended angle of 30–45° in one of these ways:

A Prop the board against the front edge of the table and rest the base in your lap.

B Place one end of the board on the table and lean the other end on books or covered bricks. Secure the board against the table edge with a thin strip of wood held in place at each end by two small clamps.

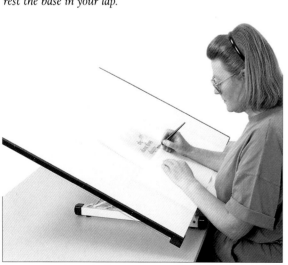

C Buy a ready-made designer's drawing board.

D Place your table against a wall and lean your board on the wall at the desired angle. Secure the board against the table edge with a thin strip of wood held in place at each end by two small clamps.

Prepare for writing by placing padding between your board and the writing paper to give springiness to your writing. You can use any paper, but blotting paper is especially suitable because its spongy texture gives the right degree of resilience. Tape one or two sheets of this to your board as shown at right.

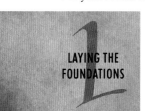

Setting up and ruling up

Keep your work in position and protect it from grease from your hand with a "guard sheet". This is a strip of thin paper — layout paper is ideal — placed across the board and attached on either side with masking tape (see below). Slip your writing sheet under the guard sheet and move it up as you write, leaving the guard sheet fixed in position just beneath each new writing line. This will ensure that you are always writing in the best possible position. It is not a good idea to attach the writing sheet to the board, because the change in eye level and in the position of the arm as it moves down a fixed page — particularly towards the bottom where the hand is cramped — causes variations in writing. The area in which good writing is most easily achieved is about two-thirds up the board, and the guard sheet is kept just below this in order to maintain a consistently good writing position.

PREPARING THE BOARD
Tape one or two sheets of blotting paper over your board in order to achieve the best writing results.

Writing paper   Blotting paper

Board   Masking tape

USING A GUARD SHEET
Tape a guard sheet to your board to protect your work. Do not tape down your writing sheet, so that you can easily adjust its position under the guard sheet as you work.

20

USING A RULER AND SET SQUARE

Calligraphy grids and pre-ruled papers can be slipped under a transparent writing surface for practice in the early stages, but it is a good idea to get into the habit of ruling your own lines as soon as possible. Pre-ruled lines can be restricting and may not give accurate results. To guide your writing, you will need to rule straight and accurately spaced lines. Using a set square and ruler will help to keep the lines parallel. The photographs below show you what to do. Alternatively, you can use a T-square to draw your writing lines (see p. 46). Align the end of the T-square with the left edge of your board and slide it up or down to the required position. Additional information on ruling writing lines can be found on pages 46–47.

1 *Place the ruler along the left-hand edge of the paper. Hold the set square against the ruler, and slide it up to the top edge of the paper. If the top edge of the set square does not align with the paper, the paper is not square and should be trimmed accordingly.*

2 *Place the ruler along the top edge of the paper. Slide the top edge of the set square along the ruler until the left-hand edge of the set square is in the position in which you wish to place your left margin. Lightly rule the margin in pencil.*

3 *Place the ruler along the ruled left margin. Slide the set square down the ruler until the top edge is in the position in which you wish to place your first writing line. Lightly rule a line. Continue to move the set square down the ruler and rule as many lines as you need.*

LINE SPACING AND MARGINS

A block of writing looks better if it has a margin around it to set it off. It is usual to have an equal measurement at the top and sides (A), with double this (2 × A) at the bottom margin.

The distance between writing lines (interline space) is determined by the x height of the letters. This is the height of the body of a lowercase (minuscule) letter, excluding ascenders or descenders (tops and tails on letters such as b and p); (see "Letter height", p. 24). Sufficient space must be left between writing lines, however, to accommodate ascenders and descenders without their becoming entangled. A distance three times the x height from baseline to baseline is usually best for beginners when starting to use lowercase letters. See page 44 for further advice on calculating margins for different pieces of work.

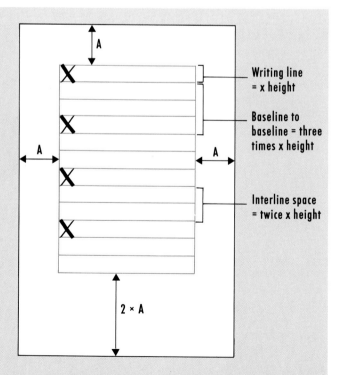

Writing line = x height

Baseline to baseline = three times x height

Interline space = twice x height

A first alphabet

LAYING THE FOUNDATIONS

For your first calligraphy, work with a simple but interesting script. The lowercase alphabet used here, based on the circle, is an excellent starting point and, when written rhythmically, forms a useful and attractive script. This script is chosen largely because of its legibility to the modern reader, accustomed to the square capitals and rounded lowercase letters of printed Roman type. The clear relationship between the letterforms of this foundational hand makes it an ideal introduction to calligraphy and one that forms a useful basis for all calligraphic work.

The key features of the foundational alphabet, in its pencil-drawn form, are shown on the facing page. Look at these before you begin writing to give yourself an over-view of the characteristics of this script.

A good way to learn any script is to practise the letters first in pencil in their skeleton form — without thicks and thins. This enables you to establish and understand the letter proportions and shapes and their relationship to one another. Getting the feel of the script and fixing the basic letterforms firmly in your mind at this stage will make the use of the edged pen easier and more successful.

QUOTATION FROM HAMLET
Gareth Colgan

Here a foundational (roundhand) hand is written with energy and rhythm to produce a dramatic interpretation of the text. Even straightforward letterforms have the potential to produce calligraphic work of great quality. Dimensions: 33 cm × 58.5 cm (13" × 23").

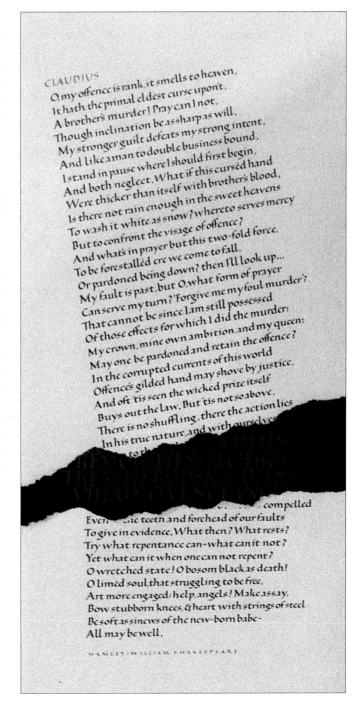

CLAUDIUS

O, my offence is rank, it smells to heaven,
It hath the primal eldest curse upon't,
A brother's murder! Pray can I not,
Though inclination be as sharp as will.
My stronger guilt defeats my strong intent,
And like a man to double business bound,
I stand in pause where I shall first begin,
And both neglect. What if this cursed hand
Were thicker than itself with brother's blood,
Is there not rain enough in the sweet heavens
To wash it white as snow? Whereto serves mercy
But to confront the visage of offence?
And what's in prayer but this two-fold force,
To be forestalled ere we come to fall,
Or pardoned being down? then I'll look up...
My fault is past. But O, what form of prayer
Can serve my turn? 'Forgive me my foul murder'?
That cannot be since I am still possessed
Of those effects for which I did the murder,
My crown, mine own ambition, and my queen:
May one be pardoned and retain the offence?
In the corrupted currents of this world
Offence's gilded hand may shove by justice,
And oft 'tis seen the wicked prize itself
Buys out the law. But 'tis not so above.
There is no shuffling, there the action lies
In his true nature, and with ourselves

compelled
Even to the teeth and forehead of our faults
To give in evidence. What then? What rests?
Try what repentance can - what can it not?
Yet what can it when one can not repent?
O wretched state! O bosom black as death!
O limed soul, that struggling to be free,
Art more engaged! help, angels! Make assay,
Bow stubborn knees, & heart with strings of steel
Be soft as sinews of the new-born babe -
All may be well.

HAMLET: WILLIAM SHAKESPEARE

GEOMETRIC FORMS

Foundational letterforms are founded on the concept of a circle within a square, as shown in the diagrams at right. You do not need to draw the letters geometrically, but an awareness of these underlying principles will help you understand the structure and proportions of the letterforms and provide a useful reference when you are writing the letters freehand in the exercises that come later.

Although each letter of the alphabet is different, groups of letters share common elements and the same strokes frequently recur. The quickest and easiest way to learn, therefore, is to practise letters in groups of similar formation and width. Most foundational letters are three-quarters the width of the circle on which they are founded (see facing page), and they belong to four formation groups (right). The letters in the formation-group diagrams are the same size as those you will be writing. It may be helpful to trace them once or twice first. Numerals and arrows show the order in which you should write your strokes and the direction in which to move your pencil. When you come to writing the letters freehand, modifications will be needed to c, d, e, and x, for aesthetic reasons. These are indicated in the skeleton alphabet (p. 26). Have a look at this and refer once more to the geometric diagrams before you begin to practise the formation groups shown on the next page.

Straight-sided arched letters: n, m, h, r, a, plus i. These are three-quarter-width, except m (which is double this width), and i (which is a single stroke with no substantial width).

Circular letters: g, c, e, d, q, b, p, o. These are seven-eighth-width, except the fully circular o and g (which is based on a smaller o).

Letters containing diagonals: k, v, w, y, x, z. These are three-quarter-width, except w (which is double this width).

Letters with related top and tail curves: f, s, j. These are three-quarter-width.

Straight-sided letters with related base curve: l, t, u. These are three-quarter-width.

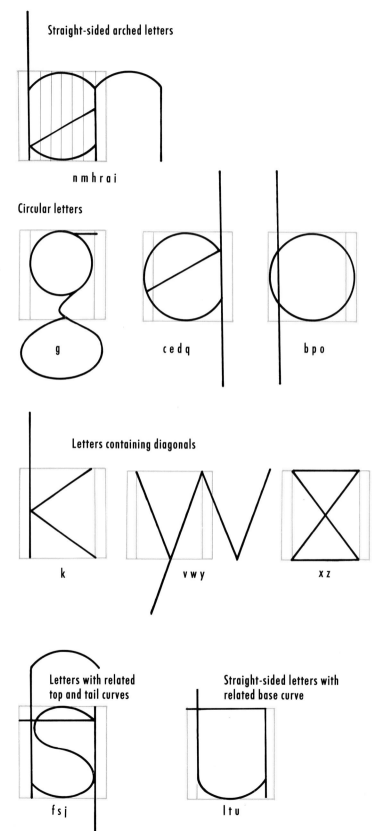

Straight-sided arched letters

n m h r a i

Circular letters

g   c e d q   b p o

Letters containing diagonals

k   v w y   x z

Letters with related top and tail curves

f s j

Straight-sided letters with related base curve

l t u

LETTER HEIGHT

Before practising even the most basic script, you will need to have some understanding of the size and proportions of the letters. For a lowercase script the key measurement is the x height. This is the height of the main part, or body, of the letter, excluding ascenders and descenders (see right). The height of capital scripts is defined by the overall height of the letters. For most of the exercises in this section, the letters should be written to an x height of 13 mm ($^1/_2$"). Ascenders and descenders are slightly shorter.

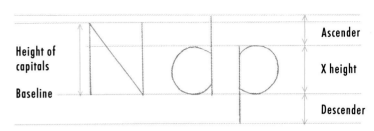

LETTER-FORMATION GROUPS

Before attempting to write a foundational hand with an edged pen, practise the formation groups in pencil as shown below.

1 *Using an HB pencil, rule your practice sheet with lines 13 mm ($^1/_2$") apart.*

2 *Leave two blank lines between each writing line, or arrange the groups as shown in the model, to avoid the collision of ascenders and descenders.*

3 *Refer to the diagrams (p. 23) to remind yourself how the letters relate to the square and the circular o. The alphabet on p. 26 gives further information about the forms of individual letters.*

4 *The letters shown below in group order can be traced so that you get the feel of them. Take care to follow the correct stroke order.*

5 *Write the letters freehand, group by group, in HB pencil. Repeat each group several times before moving on to the next.*

6 *Check the letters against the model after each writing. You will use the same sequence when you write with the pen.*

7 *Draw the letters firmly. Correct the shapes as you go, erasing if necessary. Your aim is to get an understanding of the structure and relationship of the letter shapes. This may entail a number of attempts.*

ALTERNATIVE LETTERFORMS

The letterforms shown on the previous page are the standard ones for foundational hand. However, some letters can be rendered in a different way. The choice is a matter for the individual calligrapher. Some common alternative forms are shown at right with guidance as to stroke order and direction. Try these when you feel confident with the standard alphabet.

SPACING AND THE RULE OF THREE

The aim of spacing in most calligraphic scripts is to make the areas of space within and between letters appear equal. If all letters were straight-sided, this would be easy — you could simply measure the same amount of space between each of them. As letterforms vary, however, you need to be aware of the spacing needs of different combinations of letters.

This means thinking about the area inside each letter — the counter space — as well as the white area created around the letter itself. In practical terms, to achieve even spacing, a curved letter should be placed closer to a straight-sided letter than another straight-sided form would be, and two adjacent curved letters should be placed closest of all.

Spacing patterns for each script can be established with the aid of a key diagram (see right). Using this diagram, you can verify the amount of space needed to achieve a balanced effect.

A helpful way to check your spacing is with the "Rule of Three". Look at the first three letters in your writing (of the alphabet or a word) and see whether the space on either side of the middle letter appears equal. Then, looking at the last two letters of that trio and the following letter, verify the spacing on either side of the new middle letter. Continue in the same fashion until you have checked the entire alphabet or word, re-writing if necessary.

You can learn the principles of even spacing between differently shaped letters by practising the following exercise.

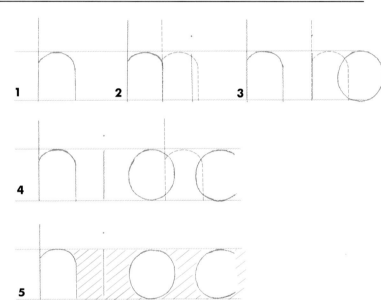

1 *Rule lines in pencil 13 mm (¹/₂″) apart.*

2 *Copy the "h i o c" diagram above in pencil, using the following guidelines.*

3 *Write the h, ensuring that it is the correct width because it will determine the spacing pattern. Place an i next to it, slightly closer than the width of the h counter (the space inside the h).*

4 *Write an o slightly closer to the i. To maintain the appearance of equal space, adjacent straight-sided and curved letters need to be closer than a pair of straight-sided letters.*

5 *Place the c even nearer to the o, because adjacent curved letters let in additional space between them at top and bottom.*

25

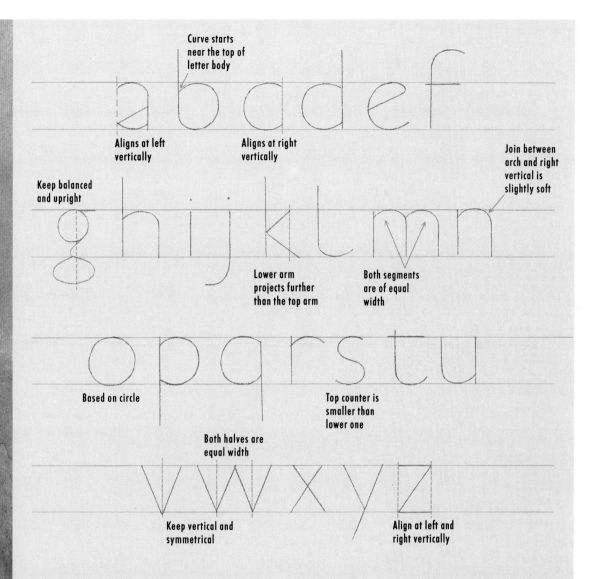

Curve starts
near the top of
letter body

Aligns at left
vertically

Aligns at right
vertically

Join between
arch and right
vertical is
slightly soft

Keep balanced
and upright

Lower arm
projects further
than the top arm

Both segments
are of equal
width

Based on circle

Top counter is
smaller than
lower one

Both halves are
equal width

Keep vertical and
symmetrical

Align at left and
right vertically

Use the knowledge acquired through practising letter groups and spacing to write and space the full skeleton foundational alphabet. Do not be held back by faults in letterforms and spacing on the first attempt, but consider where you could make improvements before you try again. Work on lines ruled 13 mm ($^1/_2$″) apart and copy the alphabet in sections (a-f, g-n, o-u, v-z), spacing the letters as evenly as possible.

CHECKLIST
✔ Letters should not slant.
✔ Letter bodies (except g) should fill the space between lines.
✔ b, d, p and q have curves based on the circular o and should contain an equal area within the counter.
✔ The arches of h, m, n, a and r should reflect the circular o.
✔ Base curves of t and u reflect the circular o.
✔ Crossbars of t and f are at the level of the x height.

WORD PRACTICE

A good way to get used to spacing is to check and re-write the same few words. Words containing mainly straight-sided letters are spaced equidistantly. Concentrated practice with repeated letter combinations will not only help you achieve even spacing, but will develop your ability to judge and improve your spacing with unfamiliar texts. For spacing between words, you should leave room for an o of the script being written, so in this case make the space between words the width of a foundational-script o.

1 *Rule lines 13 mm (¹/₂″) apart.*

2 *Write the words shown.*

3 *Check the letterforms and spacing, and repeat as necessary to correct any errors.*

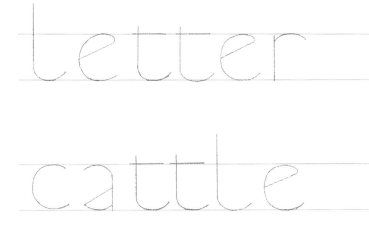

Using coloured pencils

Even at this early stage in your knowledge of calligraphy, you can aim to produce attractive finished work. Try using coloured pencils for uncomplicated projects, such as the labels for storage jars shown here. The foundational script with its clear and legible letterforms is ideal for this purpose. A simple decorative border provides the finishing touch.

1 *Rule the writing lines to the desired height, and write the words in pencil to allow letterforms and spacing to be checked and corrected if necessary.*

2 *The final versions, written in coloured pencil, have borders worked in gouache. Care is needed to ensure the correct placement of the border around the text.*

The basics of edged-pen calligraphy

Tools and materials

THE BASICS OF EDGED-PEN CALLIGRAPHY

The increasing popularity of calligraphy has brought with it a huge range of writing tools and materials. The variety may seem confusing at first, but bear in mind that the only additions to your basic equipment (pp. 16–17) that you really need are pen and ink.

The essential tool for most pen-written calligraphy is a pen with a broad-edged nib. That is why calligraphy is sometimes termed "the art of the edged pen". To write accurate strokes you have to keep the entire edge of the nib consistently in contact with the paper. This can feel awkward at first, and it may help to spend a little time practising with a double pencil (below left), whose twin points produce the same effect as the edged nib with an outline form. Alternatively, you can use a broad-edged carpenter's (chisel) pencil (below right), sharpened to a chisel shape, which reproduces the action of the edged pen even more directly. Choose a medium to soft grade, or the type made for drawing, which will not need to be pressed too hard to make a mark.

NIBS

Mitchell roundhand nibs are made in sizes 0–6, including some half-sizes. The lower the number, the broader the nib. Other makes use different sizing systems (see "Checking your nib size", p. 33). Left-oblique nibs, for left-handed calligraphers, are shown below left.

DOUBLE PENCILS

Make your own double pencils by binding together two HB pencils with a rubber band or masking tape. The points can be brought closer by shaving one side of each pencil with a sharp craft knife — keeping the cut areas level and not exposing the lead — before binding them firmly using masking tape with the points aligned. (For left-handers, the right point should be slightly higher.)

CARPENTER'S PENCIL

A flat carpenter's (chisel) pencil can be sharpened into the shape of a broad nib. This is very useful for practising weighted letterforms.

PEN-HOLDERS

Some calligraphers find rounded pen-holders more comfortable to hold than faceted ones.

FOUNTAIN PENS

With their large-capacity reservoirs, fountain pens are useful for the beginner, who can practise without constantly having to refill the pen. Fountain-pen sets come with a range of nib sizes.

The many varieties of edged pen fall into two main categories: the pen you assemble (also known as a dip pen), consisting of a holder and a steel nib, usually with a reservoir that fits above or beneath it; and the fountain pen with a built-in reservoir. The function of the reservoir is to extend the flow of ink by storing it and feeding it steadily to the nib edge. Fountain pens have large-capacity reservoirs, which do not need to be constantly refilled. They are useful when practising and for travelling. They can be purchased as a set that includes interchangeable nibs of different sizes. A fountain pen with a squeeze- or piston-fill reservoir is preferable to a cartridge refill, which limits changes of ink colour. The pen should be kept meticulously clean to allow the ink to flow freely.

Continued on page 33 ▷

RESERVOIRS

Most small clip-on reservoirs fit on the backs of the nibs used with assembled pens.

SHARPENING STONE

Fine-grain Arkansas stone is used to keep pen nibs sharp, so that hairline cross-strokes can be achieved.

PAINTBRUSH

An old watercolour brush is useful for loading ink or paint into the pen.

AUTOMATIC PENS

These extra-broad writing edges can be used for large script such as headings, display work such as posters, or for pattern making and decoration. Their nibs have two flat halves, and the gap in between acts as a built-in reservoir.

COIT PENS

Coit pens are used for large lettering, borders and decoration. The nibs are split in a variety of widths so that the thick strokes of the letter are divided.

Assembling the pen

One of the advantages of assembling a pen is that you can adjust it to suit your individual requirements. Dismantling, cleaning and re-assembling it regularly will also help you become well acquainted with your writing instrument. The assembled pen shown here is the standard pen used for teaching the scripts throughout this book.

1 Ease the nib into the holder. Avoid putting pressure on the writing edge. Slide the nib in as far as possible. It should fit closely to the holder's neck.

2 With a new nib, be sure to remove the protective lacquer coating. Plunge it into hot water, or hold it briefly in a flame and then cool it in cold water.

3 Place a sharpening stone on a flat surface and lubricate it with water. Place the nib at 30°, with the top towards the stone and the underside of the nib facing you.

4 Keeping the nib at 30°, move it across the stone 10–12 times. Check the sloping edge of the nib under a magnifying glass and sharpen it with the top of the nib facing you until it is even.

5 It may be necessary to fit the reservoir by first loosening the side flaps with slight pressure from your finger and thumb so that it can slide easily on to the nib.

6 The reservoir should make just enough contact to prevent it from falling off. It must not grip the nib so tightly that it distorts the writing edge.

7 The reservoir should be positioned about 3 mm (¹⁄₈″) from the writing edge, or slightly further back on smaller nib sizes.

8 If the reservoir is too far forward, it will catch the paper and drag ink across the surface; if too far back, it will not supply ink to the writing edge.

HANDMADE PENS

It is easy to make your own pens from a fine piece of bamboo. Such pens can produce interesting and highly individual lettering effects.

Calligraphic felt-tip pens with broad, chisel-shaped tips are useful for planning layout ideas, but are not normally used for finished work, where accuracy and clear lines are essential.

You can get good results from either fountain or assembled pens, and it is important to choose the type of pen with which you feel most comfortable. Sooner or later, however, you will probably want to try the pen-holder, nib and reservoir that you assemble yourself. This is because of the flexibility offered by the vast range of nibs. It is also easier to change colour and to wash nibs, and you can regularly check all the working parts.

Cleaning the pen

Taking care of your tools can become an enjoyable part of the whole craft, not a chore. A pen must be kept clean to perform well. Nibs left with ink or paint drying in their recesses will clog and rust. Rust will also develop on pen-holders left to soak in water with their nibs attached. When writing is finished, the pen-holder, nib, and reservoir need to be separated, washed and dried.

1 *Ease the reservoir off the nib and soak in a bowl of lukewarm soapy water. If it is stuck, do not force it. This may damage the nib. Soak it first to loosen any dried ink.*

2 *Dip an old toothbrush in the lukewarm water, and gently scrub both sides of the nib and reservoir.*

3 *Immediately after washing, dry the nib and reservoir with a cotton rag. Do not use tissues, which leave fibres.*

CHECKING YOUR NIB SIZE

Throughout this book, the nib sizes quoted refer to Mitchell roundhand nibs, which are widely used by calligraphers. If you are using a different brand, you will need to convert these sizes to those of your nib. A simple way of doing this is to hold each of your nibs against the size checker below to determine which Mitchell size it most closely matches.

0

1

1½

2

2½

3

3½

4

5

6

To produce the sharp strokes that characterize calligraphy, your pen and your ink must be compatible. The inks used by medieval scribes (often composed of lampblack — a kind of soot — mixed with gum and water) were efficient and durable, as surviving manuscripts testify. However, inks that had been suitable

Inks and paints

for quills frequently corroded metal pens, and during the 19th century alternative inks were developed. Some calligraphers continue to make inks from old recipes for creative purposes, but nowadays there are a great number of prepared inks from which to choose, offering a variety of properties.

It is fun to experiment with inks once you have gained confidence, but for now there are only two factors to consider. The ink must flow smoothly and be an intense black, even when dry. Some inks appear black at the time of writing, but dry to a disappointing grey. For smooth flow, the ink must be non-waterproof.

You can buy non-waterproof ink ready for use or in a thick solution to be diluted with water. Use distilled water, not water from the tap, or the ink will deteriorate. Remember to keep the lid on, so that the ink does not dry around the top of the bottle and flake into the liquid. Always shake the bottle or stir the ink before starting to write, and, if you write for a long period, stir the ink occasionally.

The introduction of colour in the pen strokes or background opens up a vast range of creative possibilities. The methods used are easily within the reach of the beginner. The paints generally used by calligraphers are artists' watercolours, gouache (an opaque form of watercolour) and some liquid acrylics.

INKS
Both the black calligraphers' ink you use and the coloured inks should be non-waterproof, as the shellac in waterproof inks can clog the pen.

LIQUID ACRYLICS
Only water-based paints are suitable for use in the pen. Liquid acrylics mix better than acrylics from a tube.

PALETTE
Mix your paint on a palette. Use distilled water if you plan to store the paint.

If you fill your pen by dipping it directly into the ink or paint, it will be hard to control the amount of liquid in the reservoir, and you may get drips on your paper. It is therefore advisable to use a brush to feed ink or paint directly into the reservoir. Always make sure there is no ink or paint on the upper surface of the nib.

USING INK

Fill a medium-size paintbrush with ink. With the brush in one hand and the pen in the other, feed the ink in from one side, between the nib and the reservoir. A dropper may be used instead of a brush to load ink into the reservoir.

USING PAINT

1 Squeeze out about 6 mm (¹⁄₄″) of paint or gouache. Add water and blend thoroughly with a soft paintbrush until the mixture is the consistency of ink.

2 Load the reservoir with the paint using a brush.

3 Test the paint flow on a piece of scrap paper. If the paint is too thin, the colour will not be strong enough. If the paint is too thick, it will clog the pen.

4 Be sure to mix enough paint to complete the job. A change to a new batch of colour halfway through is likely to show.

WATERCOLOURS
Paint from a tube, rather than a pan, is easier to handle and mix in quantity.

GOUACHE
Gouache is an opaque watercolour, and is frequently used in calligraphy.

Paper makes a great contribution to the mood, direction and success of the work produced on it. By getting to know some of the many types of paper available, and how they behave with different nibs, you will be able to increase the accuracy of your writing.

Medieval manuscripts were written on

Paper

Build a collection of samples of papers that interest you, storing them in a folder. Remember to label each paper, and annotate it with observations on how it affects nib movement and how it interacts with ink and paint.

parchment or its finer-quality counterpart, vellum — both durable surfaces made from animal skin. Printing brought about the development of paper made from vegetable fibres. Today, calligraphers choose their papers from three main categories: handmade, mould-made and machine-made. Most papers have a range of finishes: hot-pressed (the smoothest surface), Not (which has more of a tooth) and rough (which has a very textural surface).

Handmade papers are made by dipping a mesh-covered frame, known as a mould, into a solution of fibres. These are held in place on the mould by another frame called a deckle, which gives its name to the distinctive wavy edges of a handmade sheet. The same materials are used to produce mould-made papers, but the process is speeded by a cylinder-mould machine, which produces the paper as a continuous roll. The quality of mould-made paper is close to that of handmade sheets, but there are only two deckle edges, and machine production usually makes them less expensive.

Machine-made papers are mass-produced. Their main advantage is their low cost. Many machine-made papers are suitable for calligraphy and artwork. Machine-made papers are especially useful for practising and planning, to avoid wasting expensive paper.

CHOOSING PAPERS

When choosing paper, you need to consider its weight and its surface. The weight, which indicates the thickness, is especially important when using painted backgrounds (see pp. 124–

Becoming familiar with different types of paper will enable you to choose the best surface for your work. Knowing the cause of paper problems can be helpful.

SURFACE TOO ROUGH

Ink flow is impeded and it is difficult to guide the nib steadily and smoothly.

SURFACE TOO SLIPPERY

The nib cannot be controlled. Ink builds up on the surface and may run into lower lines.

UNSIZED, OR WATERLEAF, PAPER

Absorbs ink or paint like blotting paper.

TEXTURED PAPER

Surface bumps may distort writing, and may contain hairs that are picked up by the nib.

UNEVEN SIZING

This causes the letters to "bleed" in patches.

GREASY SURFACE

This resists the writing medium. Grease spots can cause the same problem.

7). Surfaces are graded as hot-pressed, cold-pressed, or rough, according to the processes used to dry the paper. Porosity is affected by the addition to the paper of a gluey substance known as size. Unsized or poorly sized papers allow ink or paint to spread, or "bleed," into the fibres, and too much size can make the surface too resistant. Test a paper's suitability by trying it out with the pen: if the surface drags or catches in the nib, or the ink bleeds, it is probably unsuitable. However, certain surface difficulties can be overcome (see "Surface preparation", below). Highly coated, glossy papers should be rejected; the ink is likely to stand in blobs on the surface.

SELECTING THE TOP SIDE

Papers sometimes have different surfaces on different sides. The top side usually has a smoother finish. With watermarked papers, you can find out which is the top side by holding the paper up to the light and looking for the watermark. If it reads properly, the top side is toward you.

SURFACE PREPARATION

You can improve writing sharpness on porous or greasy papers by sealing the surface with a special fixative spray or with gum sandarac, a traditional material favored by many calligraphers. Gum sandarac is bought in crystals. Grind these to a fine powder with a mortar and pestle. Place the powder in a square of clean fine white cotton, gather the corners of the square together, and tie at the neck to form a little bundle. Shake this gently to allow a light dusting of powder to fall on your paper. Too much will mar the writing, so take care to blow away any excess.

Handmade paper

Cold-pressed paper

Hot-pressed paper

Pastel paper

Mould-made pastel paper

Cover paper

It is important to establish a relaxed, yet firm and steady way of holding the pen that also enables you easily to change the pen angle when needed. Most calligraphers rest the pen on the first joint of the middle finger, and use the thumb and forefinger to guide the pen and maintain its angle. The hold should be fairly

THE BASICS OF EDGED-PEN CALLIGRAPHY

Holding the pen

The simplest way of altering the angle of the nib with minimum disruption to writing flow is to roll the pen between your thumb and forefinger without altering the position of your hand. In the illustrations you will see how the angle of the pen-holder held in your hand moves in a 90° arc as you change the angle of the nib from 0° through 45° to 90°.

0°

close to the nib, as this unifies the writer and the writing instrument. It is also important to push the nib well down into the holder to aid control. This approach is used for any broad-edged writing instrument.

Pen-angle problems are more marked in the early stages of learning. A flatter angle to the writing line is more natural than a steep one, so you will need to check the angle constantly at first. You also need to ensure that your pen-holder is held at the correct angle to your writing surface to facilitate smooth writing — 40°–60° is best (see below right).

45°

90°

ANGLE OF PEN TO BOARD
Establish an angle of 40°–60° between your pen and board for best results. In this picture, you can see how the heel of the hand rests on the board to ensure stability.

RIGHT-HANDED HOLD
Most right-handers find it easy to adopt a position in which the pen is held lightly but firmly between the thumb and forefinger and rests on the first joint of the middle finger.

HINTS FOR LEFT-HANDERS

For most scripts, the strokes are pull, rather than push, strokes — that is, the pen is pulled across the paper instead of being pushed. These standard stroke directions are aimed at right-handers. In order to follow the correct stroke direction, left-handed calligraphers cannot simply use a mirror image of the right-handed writing positions, but have to adopt alternative positions for their writing hand and arm.

Left-handed calligraphers have discovered many ways of overcoming this difficulty, but the under-arm position shown at right is recommended. This position enables strokes to be the same as for right-handers, and the work can be viewed from a normal perspective. Pen-holder and nib are aligned in a similar way to the right-handed pen — an obvious advantage when learning from a right-handed teacher. However, this position may not suit all left-handed calligraphers. Alternative positions are shown in the panel below right. You may need to experiment with different methods before you find the solution that is best for you.

A more general difficulty encountered by left-handers is achieving and maintaining a steep enough pen angle to the paper. Some people solve this by slanting the paper up to the left, but this may disturb the writing of verticals and constant slopes. Oblique nibs (shown on page 30) can help left-handers to achieve accurate angles.

Do not be discouraged if it takes a little time to find a way of writing comfortably; many successful calligraphers are left-handed, and there are satisfactory solutions to most individual difficulties. Talking to other left-handers and watching demonstrations may help. It is important to remember, however, that most early problems in calligraphy are common to both left- and right-handers.

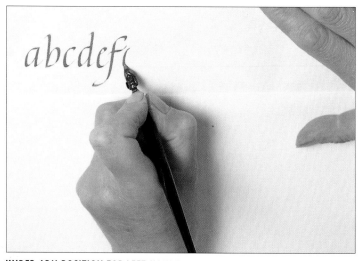

UNDER-ARM POSITION FOR LEFT-HANDERS

At the wrist, turn the left hand as far as possible to the left in order to place the nib on the paper at the correct angle. It may help to slant your paper down to the right. Encourage free arm movement by placing the paper slightly to the left of your body and writing from this position. It will help if you work on an extra-wide board with a guard sheet across the full width, so that you can move your work to the left once or twice per line as you write.

ALTERNATIVE LEFT-HAND POSITIONS

If for any reason the under-arm position does not suit you, try one of the alternatives shown here.

HOOK POSITION

Place your hand above the writing line in a "hook" position by flexing the wrist downward. Then, after placing the nib on the paper at the desired angle, move the nib in the direction of the stroke. It may help to slant the paper slightly to the left.

VERTICAL POSITION

In this method, the paper is placed at 90° to the horizontal and you work from top to bottom instead of from left to right. This enables strokes to be rendered as for right-handers, although the unusual angle may make it difficult to judge the letterforms as you work.

When you begin to write with the edged pen, one of the first questions that arises will be how to encourage, or how to control, the ink flow. Gentle pressure on the nib and small pulling strokes on a spare piece of paper will usually get the pen started. If not, check that the reservoir is in contact with the nib,

Making a mark

that the fit is not too tight, and that it is close enough to the edge of the nib (see "Assembling the pen", p. 32). If the ink flows too fast, you may simply have over-loaded the nib, in which case you can make some more pulling strokes on the spare piece of paper until the flow is correct. Alternatively, the reservoir may be fitted too close to the edge of the nib, or a new nib may not have been properly cleared of lacquer (see p. 32). Sometimes an incompatible paper or ink is the cause (see p. 36).

Try a few strokes using a Mitchell No. 0 nib, as shown on the facing page, to get the feel of the nib. Keep the nib in complete contact with the paper to avoid writing with ragged edges. Do not press too hard or you may force the nib apart and distort the thickness of the stroke. If pressure is too light, strokes may be hesitant, slightly ragged or waisted.

PEN ANGLES AND PATTERNS

You are now ready to practise holding the pen at a constant angle to achieve thick and thin strokes. Try the exercises illustrated on the following pages to develop your skills in producing consistent strokes at accurate angles.

1 *Use a protractor to help you establish the pen angles on your practice sheet.*
2 *Copy the strokes shown, checking your writing against the examples and making any necessary corrections.*

SPARSE INK FLOW
You may not be pressing hard enough. Check that the fit of the reservoir is not too tight and that it is not too far from the edge of the nib.

OVER-HEAVY INK FLOW
The nib may be overloaded, or the reservoir may be too close to the end of the nib. Check also that no lacquer is left on the nib.

CORRECT INK FLOW
The pen is working well, and produces a dense and sharp-edged stroke.

ALIGNING THE NIB TO THE PAPER

Correct

Incorrect

A clean-edged stroke depends on both edges of the nib being in contact with the paper. A ragged edge along one side of the stroke may indicate that the nib has not been aligned correctly on the paper.

FIRST STROKES

1 *Rule lines 1 cm (¹/₂″) apart, and practise downward vertical strokes with a Mitchell No. 0 nib held horizontally (0°) to the writing line.*

2 *Keeping the nib at 0°, try writing some horizontal strokes between your writing lines from left to right.*

3 *Make further horizontal strokes, but this time practise pushing them lightly up and then pulling down at the ends.*

PRACTISING HEIGHT AND SPACING

1 *With lines ruled as before, practise parallel downstrokes. Concentrate on making them the exact height of the writing lines.*

2 *Starting with a stroke at the height of the writing lines, draw parallel strokes progressively taller, then progressively smaller, as shown.*

3 *Repeat stage 2, but this time concentrate on spacing the strokes as evenly as possible.*

PRACTISING PEN ANGLES

0° *Establish the angle.*

0° *Downward vertical pull.*

0° *Left-to-right horizontal.*

0° *Vertical and horizontal.*

30° *Establish the angle.*

30° *Downward vertical.*

30° *Left-to-right horizontal.*

30° *Combined vertical and horizontal.*

PRACTISING PEN ANGLES (continued)

45° *Establish the angle.*

45° *Downward vertical.*

45° *Left-to-right horizontal.*

45° *Vertical and horizontal.*

90° *Establish the angle.*

90° *Downward vertical.*

90° *Left-to-right horizontal.*

90° *Vertical and horizontal.*

MULTIPLE-STROKE PRACTICE
Vertical strokes

Practise parallel vertical strokes between your writing lines at pen angles of 30° and 45°, as shown at right. Try to keep the spacing even between each stroke.

30°

45°

Horizontal strokes

Next, try some parallel horizontal strokes at 30° and 45° pen angles, as shown at right, again keeping the spacing even.

30°

45°

Left-to-right diagonals
Now practise parallel diagonals between your writing lines at 30° and 45°. As before, try to ensure even spacing based on 1 nib width.

30°

45°

Right-to-left diagonals
Note how diagonals drawn from right to left produce a much thinner stroke. Practise the diagonals with a pen angle of 30° and then 45°. Concentrate on achieving parallel strokes at consistent angles.

30°

45°

PRACTISING CURVED STROKES

30° – Counter-clockwise curve
Practise arcs based on half an O, as shown.

30° – Clockwise curve
Next, practise arcs in the opposite direction.

Circular O form
Now use both strokes to complete an O.

45° – Counter-clockwise curve
Practise arcs based on half an oval O, as shown.

45° – Clockwise curve
Next, practise arcs in the opposite direction.

Oval O form
Now use both strokes to complete an O.

43

When you use your writing for a finished piece of work, the margins that you choose will make an important contribution to the overall effect. To show your writing to best advantage, you need to balance the text against the space around and within it. The amount of space between the lines, between areas of text

Margins

and between heading and text helps to determine the proportions of the outer margins. Too much space weakens a design; insufficient space makes it look cramped. Generous margins are generally preferable to narrow ones, because surrounding space gives the text unity.

Many designs use the traditionally proportioned margins found in printing and picture framing, and these are easy to calculate (see facing page). Others may flout convention to achieve a particular effect. Each piece of work has its own requirements. Your ability to assess margins will gradually become intuitive.

Side margins should be equal, but the bottom margin should be larger than the top, so that the work does not appear to be slipping off the page. If a title or author's name is used, this should be considered as part of the text area when measuring margins.

As well as the more traditional margin proportions shown here, there are many other possibilities, where less-conventional margins would be appropriate to the mood and layout of the text. These include placing the text high or low on the page with exaggerated space above or below, or placing it to one side of the page. Such margins are more intuitively assessed than "traditional" margins.

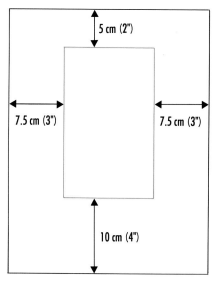

CALCULATING MARGINS: VERTICAL LAYOUT

For a vertical panel of text, the top margin is gauged by eye and doubled for the bottom margin. A measurement between these two is used for the sides. In the example above, the top is 5 cm (2"), the bottom 10 cm (4") and the sides 7.5 cm (3"). An equal measurement for the top and sides, with a deeper margin at the bottom, is sometimes appropriate (left).

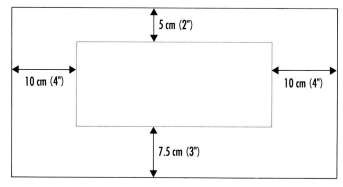

CALCULATING MARGINS: HORIZONTAL LAYOUT

For a horizontal panel of text, the widest space needs to be at the sides. In the example above, the measurements are 5 cm (2") at the top, 10 cm (4") for the sides, and 7.5 cm (3") for the bottom margin. An alternative formula is shown at left. Side margins should be equal.

Cardboard strips can be used as a framing device to help you determine the most suitable margins for your work. Make a collection of strips in varying sizes from 5 cm–10 cm (2"–4") wide: four of each width at different lengths (two long, two short). L-shaped pieces of cardboard or mountboard can also be used. You may be able to obtain scraps from a picture framer, or you could use old mounts cut into L-shapes that will, placed together, form an adjustable rectangle.

1 Place the strips, or L-shaped mounts, like a frame.

2 Here, the text is "lost" within overly wide margins. Experiment by moving the strips towards and away from the edges of the text.

3 Take care not to cramp the text between narrow side margins, as occurs here.

4 When the balance between text and white space looks right, mark the chosen margins with a light pencil point in each corner.

The hours when the mind
is absorbed by beauty
are the only hours
when we really live,
so that the longer
we can stay among
these things, so much
the more is snatched
from inevitable time

HORIZONTAL LAYOUT

In this piece (above), the space on either side of the text is filled with pale flourishes, which extend the width of the layout. The bottom margin is slightly greater than the top one, thereby "supporting" the text.

VERTICAL LAYOUT

This panel of poetry (left) achieves visually equal margins at the top and sides by the top margin being measured from the tops of the flourished ascenders and the side margins from their narrowest point.

R uling your own lines for writing will give you more precise results than guide sheets with pre-ruled lines placed under your paper. It will also provide useful practice in judging letter heights and vertical spacing. Draw the lines lightly, using a well-sharpened pencil and a metal ruler or T-square.

MEASURING BY NIB WIDTH
Write the nib-width blocks by holding the nib vertically and pulling it briefly to the right (or to the left, if you are left-handed). You can create a vertical "ladder" (right) or a "staircase" (far right).

1 *Set the dividers to the height of your "staircase" of nib widths.*

Ruling writing lines

There are several ways to rule guidelines for writing with the edged pen, and each person usually has a preferred method. None of these is complicated, but, whatever method you choose, it is important to be accurate.

The key factor is the x height (see "Letter height", p. 24). This is measured in terms of nib widths to ensure that letter proportions remain correct for the size of nib being used. The measurement is made by marking the nib widths in a series of small blocks that form a "staircase" or "ladder" of the required height (see above right). Therefore, if you are using a script written with an x height of 4 nib widths, you will build a "staircase" of four blocks to represent the height of the writing line. It is helpful to use dividers to "hold" the measurement of the x height for transfer to your writing sheet. Alternatively, you can mark it in pencil on a strip of paper.

The spacing between writing lines, called interline (or simply line) spacing, is a multiple of the x height (see p. 21). Take it from your first set of nib-width measurements, and hold it with a second pair of dividers or add it to your strip of paper. Transfer the letter-height and line-spacing measurements to your writing sheet by means of small pencilled lines — marked down both sides of the sheet to ensure accuracy. You can then rule your lines from these marks, using a ruler and set square aligned with the edge of the paper (see p. 21).

USING A T-SQUARE
A large T-square of the type shown can assist in the ruling of guidelines. As this it enables you to draw parallel lines, you need only mark the line depths along one margin.

2 *Place the dividers on a previously marked guideline indicating the top of your first line, and mark the baseline at each margin. Rule the baseline.*

Ruling your writing sheet

The method of measuring writing lines in nib widths is the best way of ensuring accurate letter proportions. Save time by making a collection of marker strips for different scripts and nib sizes to re-use when ruling writing lines.

1 *Line up a strip of paper with the top edge and left margin of your paper, and mark the position of the top of the x height on both the paper and strip.*

2 *Mark the right margin in the same way, using the same marked paper strip as a guide.*

3 *Use a ruler to draw a line between the two marked margins.*

4 *Use your chosen nib to create a "staircase" or "ladder" guide for the x height — in this case 3 nib widths — on a piece of scrap paper.*

5 *Place the paper strip used above against the ladder, aligning the marked point with the top. Mark the base of the x height on the strip.*

6 *Place the strip on the paper with the top mark aligned with the line you previously ruled. Mark the baseline on the left and right margins, and rule a line across.*

7 *Mark the interline space on the strip beneath the x-height guide. Try measuring multiples of the x height you have already marked.*

8 *Using the interline space mark on your paper strip, mark the top of the x height for the next line on both margins and rule this on the paper. Continue marking the x height and the interline spaces for the required number of lines.*

L ayout is the arrangement of text (and any illustration) on the page. The aim is to bring together the visual and textual content of the work in a way that is attractive, harmonious and legible. To some extent, layout will be dictated by the purpose of the work, the degree of formality or freedom involved, and the mood

Layout
basics

that is sought. No single format will suit every case. Creative decisions always depend upon individual judgement. This is an exciting area for discovery, but there are formulae and guidelines to help you.

Layouts can have a vertical or horizontal shape, and text may be aligned left, aligned right, justified, centred or asymmetrical (see facing page). Deciding which arrangement to choose means considering the overall texture of a piece of work in terms of positive and negative shapes — marks on the page and the spaces between them. Accustom your eye to looking for weak features when planning your layout, and aim for positive rather than understated contrasts, such as large and small, dark and light, strong and weak.

The choice of layout also depends on the sense and mood of the text, and the way it divides into lines. For a poem, line endings need to be kept as the poet wrote them. In interpreting prose, line breaks can be planned to enhance the meaning of the text. It is usual to have lines of five to nine words in a relatively lengthy text. In short texts, just one or two words per line can provide an interesting layout. Line spacing and the style of script — tall or laterally spreading letters — will also affect the shape of the text area. It is useful to begin by making thumbnail sketches — small, quickly delineated inspirational drawings that play with design ideas.

SIZING UP

To convert your thumbnail sketches to full-size layouts, draw a diagonal line from the bottom left corner of the thumbnail to the top right of the larger sheet, as shown in the diagram. If the measurement is twice the size of the original, for example, all measurements should double, including the nib size. An alternative method is to use a photocopying machine that records the percentage of enlargement.

CHECKLIST

Factors that affect your choice of layout:
✔ *Who is the text for?*
✔ *Where will the text be displayed?*
✔ *How much text is there?*
✔ *Are there other components — heading, subheading, author, title or date, for example?*
✔ *Is the text poetry that must retain its line scheme?*
✔ *Is the text prose, and where should line breaks come?*
✔ *How long are the lines?*
✔ *What is the meaning of the text?*
✔ *What is the mood of the text — lively, static, formal or informal, for example?*
✔ *Does the text need decoration, and of what kind?*

TYPES OF LAYOUT

CENTRED

The writing lines are balanced equally on either side of a central line (drawn faintly in pencil for guidance and erased when writing is complete). This symmetrical layout is often useful when balancing long and short lines. A centred layout is most suitable for poetry or short prose pieces.

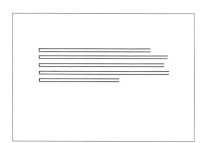

ALIGNED LEFT

All writing lines begin from a straight vertical left margin. This gives a strong left edge and a softer right-hand effect. Avoid marked variations in line length and split words. This is a versatile layout, used for both poetry and prose.

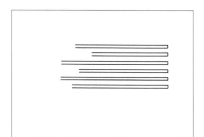

ALIGNED RIGHT

The lines are aligned vertically on the right. This layout can be effective in giving a degree of tension to a design, although it takes practice to achieve the necessary accuracy of letter widths and spacing. This layout is often seen in short texts such as letterheads.

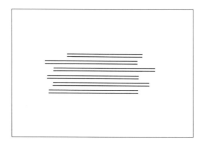

ASYMMETRICAL

This is a layout that does not conform to an established alignment and yet maintains a sense of balance. A key feature is the non-alignment of most or all line beginnings and endings. The informality of the layout lends itself to texts of all kinds where a feeling of movement is appropriate.

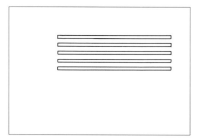

JUSTIFIED

Both right and left edges are vertically straight. Skill is needed to calculate word spacing to achieve this effect. Justified layouts produce a formal effect that is useful for prose work.

P lanning a layout and making a draft version to guide your final work is best done by the method known as "cut and paste". This avoids the process of repeatedly re-writing a text in a particular format each time a problem arises. Cutting and pasting enables you to re-assemble the text quickly and accurately in

Cutting and pasting

CUTTING-AND-PASTING EQUIPMENT
For cutting and pasting you will need a craft knife and glue. Rubber cement, which allows you to re-position the text until you are happy with the result, is the best glue for this purpose.

numerous alternative layouts. It allows you to "play" with the text and, in this way, to discover a range of approaches. Begin by writing your text on layout paper. Cut this into lines or words, and place them on a clean sheet of paper large enough to allow the text to be moved around and with adequate surrounding space for the calculation of margins (see p. 44). Move the strips around freely to evaluate different arrangements. It is a good idea to write the text twice, or to photocopy it, so that you can try alternative layouts and compare them side by side.

When you have finalized your decisions about overall shape, line length and spacing, rule writing lines at the chosen height and paste the text in place. You now have a rough paste-up from which to copy your finished work. A step-by-step demonstration of the cut-and-paste method is shown on the facing page.

To centre text during the cut-and-paste stage of layout planning (see p. 48), fold each cut line of writing in half, so that the first and last letters cover each other. Then align this centre fold with the vertical line at the centre of your page and paste it down. When writing the final version, take careful measurements from the centred draft layout, marking each line beginning and ending with a pencilled dot. Alternatively, use a photocopy of the centred layout text, cut and fold it line by line, and keep it directly above your work for reference while you write the text in its final version.

ASSESSING YOUR LAYOUTS

Having cut and pasted your text into a provisional layout, you need to be able to make a judgement on its merits. Train your eye to look for balance and variety in the distribution of text within your chosen margins. The illustrations in this box show examples of the types of faults for which you should be on the look-out in your own paste-ups.

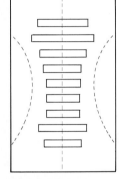

Top heavy layout

Third line too long, leaving insufficient left margin

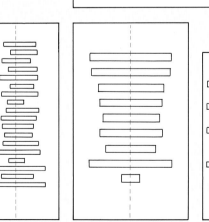

Inaccurate centring

Line lengths too similar, bottom line too short

Insufficient bottom margin

Cutting and pasting a layout

The materials needed for cutting and pasting are a sheet of layout or drawing paper measuring at least 27.5 cm × 42.5 cm (11″ × 17″), scissors, a ruler and glue such as rubber cement, which will allow you to re-position pieces of text.

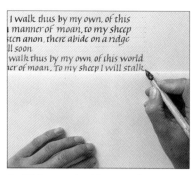

1 *Write your text in your chosen script and size. This is italic script, written at an x height of 4 nib widths.*

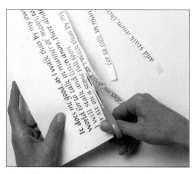

2 *When the ink is dry, cut the writing into lines using scissors or a craft knife and metal ruler.*

3 *Rule a vertical line in pencil on a sheet of layout paper, approximately 5 cm (2″) from the left edge.*

4 *Assemble the strips of writing on the sheet, beginning against the pencilled line. Move the lines to various positions across the sheet to observe the effect on shape.*

5 *Once you have decided on your preferred layout, mark and rule the lines on the layout paper.*

6 *Apply rubber cement along the writing lines.*

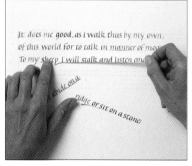

7 *Position the strips of text and press them into place. Re-positioning is possible if necessary.*

8 *When the rubber cement is dry, rub away any excess with your fingers to leave a neat and securely glued rough paste-up of your script.*

Edged-pen principles

THE BASICS OF EDGED-PEN CALLIGRAPHY

The edged pen builds up a letterform stroke by stroke, in the way that you have practised in pencil (see "Foundational hand", p. 22). However, a pen-made letter is composed of thin and thick strokes made by keeping the nib edge at a constant angle to the writing line. The width of the stroke varies according to the direction in which you move the pen while maintaining that fixed nib angle. Pen angles are specific to each script and an essential part of its individuality. A script written with a pen angle of 45°, for example, will look different from one formed mainly at 30°. Some scripts use a single pen angle and others call for changes.

KEY CHARACTERISTICS

Pen angle is not the only feature that helps to define a script. Listed opposite are eight characteristics that define and distinguish all the scripts in this book. At the start of each script you will find a panel that profiles the script in terms of these characteristics. The eight principles are therefore your key to understanding each set of letterforms.

HEIGHT AND WEIGHT

Letter height is measured in nib widths of the chosen nib size (see "Ruling writing lines", p. 46). The size of the nib and number of nib widths determine the density (or weight) of the script. There are recommended letter heights for each script based on historical examples. It is advisable to gain experience with these before exploring alternatives.

PEN ANGLE

The edged pen is held at a constant angle to achieve thick and thin lines. A recommended pen angle for each script, based on historical precedent, gives the correct distribution of weight to the letters. It may be helpful in the beginning to measure and draw the main angle of a script with a protractor (see "Making a mark", p. 40).

SLANT

All the thick downstrokes of a script, except diagonals, must slant consistently at the correct angle for that script, or letters will appear unmatched. Writing with a consistent slant is achieved by matching each successive downstroke to its predecessor, and requires practice. The correct pen angle and the correct slant must be maintained simultaneously.

ITALIC SCRIPT — Gareth Colgan

ROMAN CAPITALS — Liz Burch

SERIF FORMS

Serifs are small introductory or finishing strokes made during the construction of a letter. Their shape can vary, but must harmonize with the script. They are sometimes termed "roof and root" lines because of the repeating pattern they create along the top and bottom edges of the writing line. This pattern determines the uniformity of letters within the word shape.

O FORM

In many scripts, o is the key letter shape because the formation of the other letters is related to it. For example, in foundational hand, the arch structure of m, n and h, and the curved parts of letters such as a, b, c and d, show the roundness of the fully circular o. The same rounded shape is used for serifs. In contrast, italic is based on an oval o.

STROKE ORDER AND DIRECTION

This is the sequence in which you write the component strokes of a letter, and the direction in which the pen travels, being either pulled or pushed. It is important to follow the stroke sequence, which has evolved as a natural consequence of writing from left to right and gives optimum spacing, rhythm and flow to emerging letters.

ARCH SHAPE AND STRUCTURE

One of the main features of a lowercase (or minuscule) script is the arch structure in letters such as m, n and h. The arch shape often reflects the form of the key letter o, and stroke direction and sequence are vital to accurate arch formation. The details of arch structure are explained along with the relevant scripts.

SPEED

Certain scripts, such as foundational hand, are written slowly with many pen lifts and few push strokes, giving a characteristic formality and elegance. Others, such as italic, are written at greater speed with the pen being pulled and pushed, rarely leaving the paper, which produces a rhythmic, flowing quality. You will need to write most scripts slowly at first to get used to producing the letterforms accurately, but you will develop the right speed with practice.

53

The Arts and Crafts Movement of the late 19th and early 20th century, with its rejection of industrial methods, generated a renewal of interest in illuminated manuscripts and formal calligraphy. William Morris revived the handmade-book arts, inspired by Renaissance manuscripts, while at the turn of the century

THE BASICS OF EDGED-PEN CALLIGRAPHY

Foundational hand

PEN, BRUSH, AND INK

For your first script with the broad pen use a good quality black calligraphy ink loaded into your pen with a brush.

Edward Johnston based his early formal-penmanship studies on the 10th-century Ramsey psalter (now in the British Library). Johnston's analytical studies of letterform, and his teaching and inspiration, were responsible for bringing edged-pen calligraphy back into current usage in the 20th century. The Renaissance manuscripts and the Ramsey psalter were also very influential on other calligraphers of this period.

Today's calligraphers still find historical scripts a useful resource on which to base their own adaptations. The letter heights and pen angles recommended for the edged pen are based on those that produced the balanced proportions of traditional writing.

Pencil skeleton forms reveal the underlying structure of letters and enable you to practise stroke sequence and spacing. When you make letters with the pen, you incorporate variations of stroke weight and thickness. These are determined by the angle of the pen and the direction of your stroke. If your pen is at a 30° angle to the writing line, a straight stroke will only be as wide as the nib can make it at that angle. This will become obvious with practice, but it is essential to hold the pen at the required angle and to follow any changes in pen angle necessary for particular letters; otherwise the thick and thin parts of the letters will not have the correct width and may not be in exactly the right place.

THE RAMSEY PSALTER

This text is from an English manuscript of the late 10th century. It is one of the chief sources for modern roundhand lettering.

Ausculta, o fili, praecepta magistri,
et inclina aurem cordis tui
et admonitionem pii patris libenter evcipe et
efficaciter comple; ut ad eum per obedientiae
Laborem redeas, a quo per inobedientiae desidiam
recesseras ▾ Ad te ergo nunc mihi sermo dirigitur,
quisquis abrenuntians propriis voluntatibus,
Domino Christo vero Regi militaturus, obedientiae
fortissima atque praeclara arma sumis ✚

THE RULE OF ST BENEDICT
Joan Pilsbury

This panel, written on vellum, shows the suitability of roundhand scripts for formal work. The versal initial letter and the use of two sizes of text provide added interest. The generous interline spacing contributes to the legibility of the whole. Dimensions: 20.5 cm × 12.5 cm (8" × 5").

CHARACTERISTICS

Foundational hand is characterized by its rounded forms, based on a circular o, and vertical stems.

LETTER HEIGHT
4½ nib widths x height. Ascenders and descenders: 3 nib widths.

ARCH SHAPE AND STRUCTURE
Based on a segment of a circle, emerging high from the stem.

O FORM
Circular

PEN ANGLE
30° for most letters; 45° for left-hand diagonals of v, w, x, y. 0° for z diagonal.

STROKE ORDER AND DIRECTION
Letters are formed with frequent pen lifts and use mainly pull strokes. These characteristics help to give this script a formal quality.

SPEED
Moderate and rhythmic.

SLANT
None, keep letters vertical.

SERIF FORMS
Round hooks, echoing the circular o, are the most suitable.

DOUBLE PENCILS

One way to make the transition from pencil to pen-made forms is to practice the basic letters with double pencils. The two pencil points act like the corners of the broad nib, producing the same strokes in weighted outline form. They will help you see how thick and thin strokes form naturally as a result of the angle of the writing edge on the paper and will give you a clear demonstration of letter construction. A carpenter's (chisel) pencil can also be used for your first work with weighted letters.

1 *Prepare your pencils as shown on page 30. The points should be 6 mm (¹/₄″) apart.*
2 *Use a single pencil to rule lines 27 mm (1¹/₈″) apart.*
3 *Practice the letters shown. Hold the double pencils at 30° to the horizontal .*

FOUNDATIONAL PEN STROKES

The nib used in the foundational-hand pen exercises is a Mitchell No. 1¹/₂, which is large enough to show letter details clearly.

1 *Rule lines at an x height of 4¹/₂ nib widths of a Mitchell No. 1¹/₂ nib.*
2 *Following the diagram at right, practise the thick vertical downstrokes. Keep the pen angle at 30°, and try to achieve vertical strokes with sharp edges. All your strokes should be the same width. The width will vary if you change the pen angle or if your strokes are not vertical.*
3 *Repeat the exercise for diagonal, horizontal and curved strokes, changing the pen angle to 45° for the left-to-right diagonals. These will be used later to write v, w, x and y.*

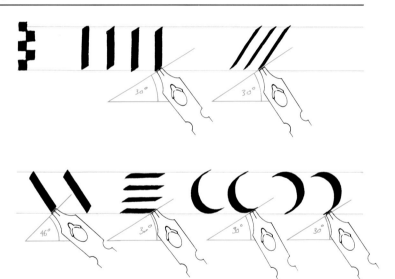

ARCHES

Arch structure is a defining feature of all lower-case scripts.

1 *Rule lines at 4¹/₂ nib widths of a Mitchell No. 1¹/₂ nib.*
2 *Make a vertical downstroke.*
3 *Place your nib completely inside the vertical as you begin the arch stroke.*

4 *Move the nib uphill to the right, keeping it almost straight until it leaves the stem. Once outside the stem, move the nib horizontally to the right, then around and down to form a circular arch with a hint of squaring at the right side where the arch and downstroke join. Make sure that your arches follow the arc of a circle.*
5 *Practise the letters n and m until you are satisfied with the result.*

LETTER-FORMATION GROUPS

Begin practising weighted letters in their formation groups, so that you get used to the movements needed to make related strokes. These groups relate to the geometric forms described on page 23.

1 *Leave two lines blank between each writing line.*
2 *Practise each group several times, following the model closely. The arrows indicate stroke order and direction. Use a 30° pen angle for all strokes except the thick diagonals of v, w, x, y (45°), and the z diagonal (0°).*
3 *Check your letters against the model after each attempt. Make sure that the letters within each group relate, exhibiting the details common to the group.*

SPACING

The principle of even spacing is the same for weighted as for skeleton foundational letters (p. 25). However, if you compare skeleton letters and weighted letters of the same height, you will notice that the weighted letters are spaced slightly closer. This is because weighted strokes take up some of the counter space (enclosed space) within letters, and so slightly less space is needed between letters.

1 *Rule lines at an x height of 4½ nib widths of a Mitchell No. 1½ nib.*
2 *Write a foundational-hand h.*
3 *Place an i next to it, slightly closer than the width of the h counter.*
4 *Place an o slightly closer to the i.*
5 *Write a c alongside the o, even closer but not touching.*

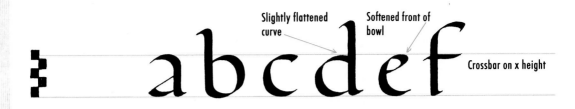

Slightly flattened curve

Softened front of bowl

Crossbar on x height

Arches based on o form

Top counter circular, lower counter oval

Right angle at join

Arch based on o form

Slightly squared-off join

Slightly flattened curve

Aligned vertically at right of letter

Slightly squared-off join

0° pen angle for diagonal

Vertical v elements

Straight right-hand diagonal

Once you are familiar with the letter groups and spacing, you are ready to write the foundational letters in alphabetical order on paper ruled at an x height of $4\frac{1}{2}$ nib widths of a Mitchell No. $1\frac{1}{2}$ nib. Write the alphabet in sections: a–f, g–n, o–u, v–z. Repeat each section several times, checking pen angle, letter shapes and spacing each time before re-writing. Use the Rule of Three (p. 25) to help you verify spacing.

CHECKLIST
✔ Keep your letters vertical.
✔ Keep your pen at an angle of 30° to the writing line, except for the thick left-hand diagonals of v, w, x and y (45°) and the z diagonal, written with a flat pen (0°).
✔ Make sure that the bodies of your letters fill the double line (except g).
✔ Check that the arches form an arc of the circular o.
✔ Make sure that stroke joins occur at the same height in letters of the same formation group, such as h, m, n and r, or q and d.
✔ Make sure that the base curves of l, t and u relate to the circular o.
✔ Check that the crossbars of t and f coincide with the top writing line. The base curve and crossbar of t should align on the right.
✔ Ensure that the two halves of m, and w, are equal.
✔ Keep ascenders and descenders 3 nib widths above and below the line (see "Characteristics", p. 55).

ALTERNATIVE FORMS AND AWKWARD JOINS

Some letters have alternative forms. If you choose an alternative, it is usually preferable to keep to it throughout a piece. Also shown are some letter combinations that sometimes cause difficulty with spacing.

1 *Rule lines at an x height of 4½ nib widths of a Mitchell No. 1½ nib.*
2 *Practise each of the letters shown in the second line.*
3 *Then practise the letter combinations shown in the second line.*

WORD PRACTICE

Once you are able to write and space the alphabet accurately, begin writing words. Trying the letterforms in new combinations will consolidate your knowledge of their shapes and extend your experience of spacing. It is best to concentrate on writing the same few words repeatedly at first. The area between words should be consistent: leave space for a foundational-hand o.

1 *Write at an x height of 4½ nib widths of a Mitchell No. 1½ nib.*
2 *Leave the width of an o between words.*
3 *Warm up by writing a line of "nini", treating it as if it were a word. Straight-sided letters are written equidistantly and are therefore easier to space.*
4 *Practise each of the words shown at right several times, checking each time for accuracy of letterform, pen angle and spacing.*
5 *Apply the Rule of Three spacing check (p. 25) to each word.*

nave

lace hall

letter

cattle

Foundational-hand greetings card

Now that you have mastered the essentials of foundational hand, you can begin to use your skills in simple decorative projects such as this attractive greetings card, written with a Mitchell No. 1½ nib and decorated with gouache applied with a pen and a brush.

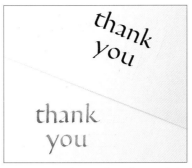

1 *Write out the words on lines ruled to 4½ nib widths. Cut and paste the lines into a centred layout (see p. 50). Copy carefully on to folded paper.*

2 *Rule margins on to the pasted-up version (see p. 44), and try out a simple border decoration in gouache. Copy the border on to your final version.*

Writing a short quotation

Planning and writing a short quotation will give you practice in rhythmic writing, spacing and design. Use a Mitchell No. 1½ nib. Write the final version over a watercolour wash in colours that echo the text.

1 *Write out your text on layout paper between lines ruled at 4½ nib widths. Do not worry about making decisions on layout at this stage.*

2 *Cut the text into individual words, and experiment with different layouts. When you have decided on a layout, paste the words into position. This then acts as a guide for the final version. A centred layout has been chosen here.*

3 *The next stage is to prepare the background. Apply a mixed watercolour wash with a large soft brush. (See also "Using colour", p. 124.) The watercolour paper used here is heavy enough not to require stretching.*

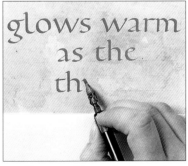

4 *Allow several hours for the wash to dry. Dust with gum sandarac (see p. 37), and lightly rule writing lines. Write the words in blue/grey gouache.*

Finished piece *The final text is an attractive piece of decorative calligraphy.*

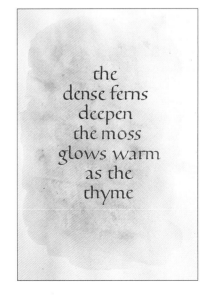

SCALING DOWN

The smaller the script, the less contrast there is between thick and thin strokes. Great precision is therefore needed when writing with small nibs. When you start to practise using small nibs, work your way gradually down the nib sizes, so that you do not lose pen control. Keep your letters at 4½ nib widths.

1 *Begin with the largest nib and practise each size in turn, writing the foundational alphabet several times, followed by words and then a short quotation.*

2 *Correct the letterforms and spacing, re-writing as necessary.*

3 *Move down a nib size only when your writing is reasonably sound.*

No. 2½ { o abcde

No. 3 { o abcde

No. 3½ { o abcde

No. 4 { o abcde

No. 5 { o abcde

WRITING LARGE

Large writing gives you practice in moving your whole arm and therefore encourages rhythmic writing. It is also helpful for detailed study of letterforms. Above all, it is fun and so encourages the flow of creative ideas. Automatic or Coit pens are ideal for large-scale writing. Large nibs devour ink and may need filling every letter, but ink can be diluted for the sake of economy when practising, or diluted paint (watercolour or gouache) can be used. Direct dipping into ink or paint may cause blobby strokes, so try filling from a large brush (see "Loading the pen", p. 35). It is important to ensure that there is no ink or paint on the front of the nib, because this may prevent sharp writing. It is usual to write with the grooved side of the nib uppermost, which gives the best flow, but writing with the grooved side down often ensures sharper strokes. Try your pen both ways, because results vary according to the individual pen and the consistency of the ink or paint. Make sure that no ink or paint dries in the nib after use. This could impede subsequent ink flow.

The best way to begin is to repeat a simple word, concentrating on forms and spacing. An interesting texture can be built up by such repetition and used later for a design. You may want to explore colour changes in the pen (see "Colour in the pen", p. 124).

COMBINING LARGE AND SMALL

Combining large- and small-scale writing can create effective contrast, but sizes must harmonize. The example at right consists of the main word written with a Mitchell No. 1 nib and subsidiary text written with a No. 3 nib. The lettering is written in gouache on a Conté-crayon background (see p. 88).

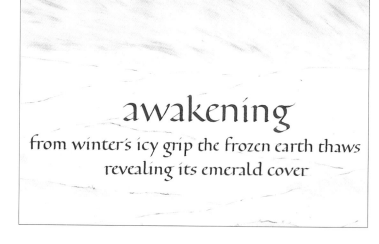

awakening
from winter's icy grip the frozen earth thaws
revealing its emerald cover

3

Mastering the letterforms

Roman capitals

The classic letterforms of ancient Rome have had a profound influence on letter design in the modern world. The Roman alphabet (based on the Greek) evolved over hundreds of years, but by the second century B.C. the Romans had established a fixed number of letters — and different ways of writing them.

Fine examples of Roman capitals are to be seen in monumental inscriptions carved in stone (in particular, those on Trajan's Column of A.D. 114). Regular, gracefully proportioned letters, the capitals were constructed according to geometric principles, using the circle, square and subdivisions of them. They were painted on to the stone with a square-edged brush before being incised with a chisel. The design of the letters, with its marked contrast of thick and thin strokes, was therefore influenced by the action of an edged tool.

There were two types of edged-pen Roman capitals used contemporaneously with inscriptional Roman capitals.

The capitals, known as *quadrata* for their square shape, were written using a square-cut reed pen or quill. They were formal and written slowly. Although they bore similarities to stone-carved capitals, many of the strokes were written at a very flat angle and with considerable manipulation of the pen.

Writing was quicker with rustic capitals (see p. 170). Written with a steep pen angle, they were characterized by thin verticals and weighty horizontals and diagonals. Rustic became the principal Roman book hand, although square capitals were often retained for headings and initial letters. Rustics were also used in painted and carved inscriptions.

Contemporary calligraphers refer directly to inscriptional letterforms as their guide for writing Roman capitals with the edged pen.

THE MOST IS DONE
Angela Swann

This text, taken from The Aeneid by Virgil, exemplifies the use of Roman capitals in a formal context. The text is written in bleedproof white gouache on watercolour paper. Dimensions: 72.5 cm × 32.5 cm (29" × 13").

MAXIMA RES EFFECTA
VIRI·TIMOR OMNIS
ABESTO QUOD SUPEREST

THE MOST IS DONE AND FOR THE REST LET ALL YOUR FEARS LIE DEAD

from The Aeneid by Virgil · translated by William Morris

THAT I AM MORTAL AND DO CONFESS MY SPAN AND A DAY BUT WHEN I GAZE ON THE
THOUSANDFOLD CIRCLING GYRE OF STARS NO LONGER DO I WALK ON EARTH BUT RISE THE PEER
OF GOD HIMSELF TO TAKE MY FILL AT THE AMBROSIAL BANQUET OF THE UNDYING

STAR-GAZING Claire Secrett

*This attractive panel of a text by Plato shows
the interest and tension created by using formal
and free writing together. Dimensions:
65.6 cm × 21.9 cm (26¼″ × 8¼″).*

*The square is the basic model for Roman capitals, with rounded
letters formed as circles or part-circles within a square.*

LETTER HEIGHT
7 nib widths.

O FORM
The O is circular.

STROKE ORDER AND DIRECTION
*All vertical and diagonal strokes
are written from top to bottom.
Horizontal strokes are from
left to right.*

SPEED
Fairly slow.

SLANT
None.

PEN ANGLE
*30° for most letters.
45° for letters containing
diagonals (A, V, W, X, Y).
Exceptions are M, N, and Z. M
and N need 50°–60° for the thin
verticals and 45° for the
diagonals, with 30° for the last
stroke of M. Z needs 30° for the
horizontals and 0° (a flat pen) for
the diagonal to give adequate
weight.*

SERIFS
*Several types of serif are suitable
for use with these letterforms,
including round hooks and
straight slabs.*

**Round hooks
top and
bottom**

**Round
hook top,
slab bottom**

**Slab
top and
bottom**

**Diagonal
line top
and bottom**

**Round
hook top,
diagonal
line bottom**

**Built-up
triangular
top, slab
bottom**

**Built-up
slab top
and bottom**

T he geometric basis of Roman capitals makes a study of their skeleton forms particularly useful. Stripped to their essential form, the skeleton letters reveal the principles that govern the shapes, proportions and underlying relationships that unify the alphabet. A knowledge of these innate characteristics

Skeleton letterforms

will help you identify the features needed to create well-shaped letterforms. The diagrams on the right show how Roman capitals are constructed on the basis of the square and a circle within the square. The letters are further analysed into formation (or family) groups on the facing page.

LETTER-FORMATION GROUPS

Roman capitals fall into four formation (or family) groups, based on the shared relationships shown in the geometric diagrams.

Wide circular letters: O, Q, C, G, D. The circular O provides the fundamental shape for this group. C, G, D are seven-eighths the width of the square.

Extra-wide letters: M, W. The M is based on a symmetrical V with its verticals slightly angled to fit exactly inside the base of the square. The base width of M equals its height. W consists of two symmetrical V's.

Three-quarter-width rectangular letters: H, A, V, N, T, U, X, Y, Z. These are based on a rectangle that is three-quarters the width of the original square.

Half-width letters: B, P, R, K, S, E, F, L. These are based on two small circles within squares, half the width and approximately half the height of the basic full-sized square. The top circle and square are slightly smaller than the bottom ones. If the letters were wider, the curved parts would be egg-shaped. I and J are also included here.

Wide circular letters

OQCGD

Extra-wide letters

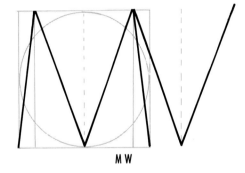

M W

Three-quarters width rectangular letters

HAV

NTUXYZ

Half-width letters

BPR

SJI

KEFL

SKELETON PRACTICE

Practise the capitals first in pencil, in their formation groups. This will give you a feel for the width of the letters. Learning the shapes and proportions, and the way in which they relate to the circular O, will prevent some of the most common mistakes that occur in pen-written Roman capitals.

1 *Rule lines 2 cm (³/₄″) apart.*
2 *Write the letters in group order, as shown below, using an HB pencil. Follow the stroke sequence indicated. Leave space between rows.*
3 *Space the letters according to the Rule of Three (see p. 25).*

WORD PRACTICE

This selection of words gives you practice with awkward letter combinations, extending your competence as well as helping you to develop your writing rhythm.

1 *Write the words shown at right in pencil between lines ruled at 2 cm (³/₄″).*
2 *Tricky combinations are TT and LL, which should not be too far apart, or adjacent diagonals, such as A V, which should not be spaced too closely.*
3 *Write each word several times, adhering closely to the model.*

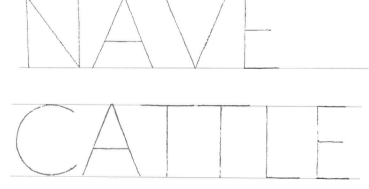

Edward Johnston described the edged pen as essentially *the* letter-making tool, and designing letters with this pen is an invaluable basis for all applied-lettering disciplines.

Before using an edged pen for your first attempts at weighted Roman capitals, try writing the letterforms with double pencils.

Weighted letterforms

The two points work like the corners of an edged-pen nib and will reveal the principles behind pen-made forms. Full instructions for making double pencils are given on page 30. Alternatively, use a carpenter's (chisel) pencil.

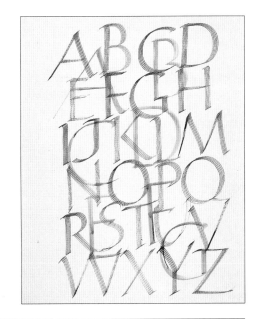

FREELY-WRITTEN ROMAN CAPITALS

DOUBLE PENCILS

Fix together two pencils so that the points are about 7 mm (⁵⁄₁₆″) apart, or use a carpenter's (chisel) pencil. This will enable you to write letters at the size shown.

1 *Rule lines 55 mm (2³⁄₁₆″) apart — the equivalent of 7 nib widths.*

2 *Hold the double pencils at the pen angles indicated for the different letters and write the letters shown at right.*

3 *Compare the result with the model, correct any mistakes and then try writing the entire alphabet, following the stroke order and direction indicated under "Letter-formation group," (see p. 66).*

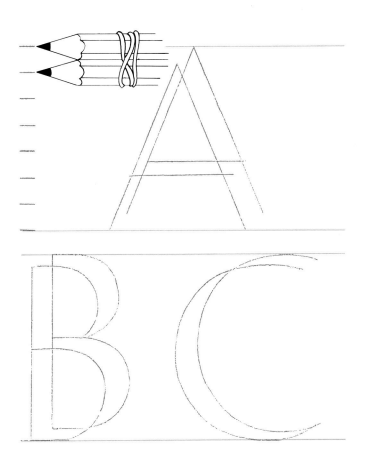

STROKE PRACTICE

Before attempting complete letters with the pen, try some of the component strokes of the weighted Roman capitals (right) to make sure your nib is working properly and to get the feel of your pen. Then review the characteristics of Roman capitals and the pen angles for producing them (see p. 61).

   In your first practice of pen-made Roman capitals, concentrate on achieving uniform basic strokes.

1 *Rule double lines at a height of 7 nib widths of a Mitchell No. 1½ nib. Using this large nib size for all the edged-pen exercises will enable you to see the stroke details clearly.*

2 *Dip your pen into the ink, shaking the surplus into the bottle, or load it from a brush (see p. 33).*

3 *Holding the pen at 30°, practise the vertical, horizontal, diagonal and curved strokes shown at right until you get the feel of the nib. Work to achieve sharp stroke edges.*

4 *Thin verticals and thick diagonal strokes need a steeper pen angle. Practise thick diagonals with a pen angle of 45° and thin verticals with a pen angle of 50°–60°.*

5 *Finally, practise large arcs that reduce the O shape at a 30° pen angle and try combining them with thick vertical strokes to form a D as shown below right.*

Thick verticals – 30° pen angle

Horizontals – 30° pen angle

Thin diagonals – 30° pen angle

Curved strokes – 30° pen angle

Thin verticals – 50°–60° pen angle

Thick diagonals – 45° pen angle

Large arcs – 30° pen angle

D form – 30° pen angle

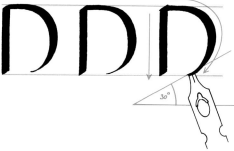

LETTER-FORMATION GROUPS

Practise the letters in their formation groups first, because faults in width will affect spacing and be more difficult to correct later. Even if the letters look satisfactory, check them carefully against the examples. Writing accurately at this stage will help you to avoid many common mistakes and enable you to progress more quickly.

1 *Write the groups as shown below between lines ruled at 7 nib widths of a Mitchell No. 1½ nib, leaving alternate lines blank.*
2 *Practise each group several times, following the model as you write each letter. The arrows indicate stroke order and direction.*
3 *Check your letters against the model after each attempt. Make sure the letters are evenly spaced.*
4 *Refer to the watchpoints on page 72 if you need further details of letter construction.*

SPACING

When spacing weighted Roman capitals, as with any script, make sure that the space inside and between letters appears equal along the writing line (see "The Rule of Three", p. 25). Weighted letters should be spaced slightly closer than skeleton letters. This is because the weight of the edged-pen nib slightly reduces the counter space (the space enclosed inside a letter) in a weighted letter, compared with that in a skeleton letter of the same height. The area between weighted letters therefore has to be correspondingly smaller to maintain the balance of spacing.

Establishing the area of space between the letters in the "H I O C" diagram will help you develop accurate, even spacing when writing with an edged pen.

1 *Rule lines to a height of 7 nib widths of a Mitchell No. 1½ nib.*

2 *Write the H and place an I next to it, slightly closer than the width of the H counter, as shown.*

3 *Place an O slightly closer still, and a C even closer. Because curved letters allow slightly more space between letters at the top and bottom, they need to be placed a little closer to adjacent letters to create equal inter-letter space.*

4 *Rewrite the "H I O C" diagram several times (shading the area between the letters) to check that you can reproduce the same letter widths and spacing each time.*

SERIFS

Now is the time to choose the serif to match your letters. A number of serifs are suitable for use with Roman capitals, ranging from the classical to the informal. Round hooks are the simplest and a good first choice. They should be restrained and relate to the circular O. Once you have practised these and feel comfortable writing sequences of words in weighted capitals, try using other serifs. Two variations are shown below.

Slab serifs should be straight, relatively short and centred at the top and bottom of vertical stems. The pen angle should be no steeper than 30° or the serifs will become too chunky. A slightly flatter angle is needed for serifs on the thin strokes of A, M, and N to keep them light enough for the stem weight.

1 *Practise verticals with a round-hook serif, top and bottom.*

2 *When you feel comfortable with these, practise writing other letters and words incorporating serifs.*

3 *Try the serif variations shown below on different letters.*

Round hooks top and bottom   **Built-up triangular top, slab bottom**   **Built-up slab top and bottom**

ABCDEFG

| Crossbar below centre | Crossbar above centre | Curves joined smoothly, strokes aligned at right | Curves joined smoothly | Crossbar at or slightly above centre | Crossbar at or slightly below centre | Vertical starts below centre |

HIJKLMN

| Crossbar above centre | Curves joined smoothly | Right-angled intersection above centre | Vertical and symmetrical "V" shape | Steepened pen angle for verticals |

OPQRSTU

| Curves joined smoothly | Crossbar at or slightly below centre | | Crossbar at centre | Aligned at right |

VWXYZ

| Symmetrical and centred on a vertical axis | Vertical and symmetrical "V" shapes | Diagonals intersect above centre | Diagonals intersect at centre | Horizontals align at left and right |

Now try the letters in alphabetical order at the same size, spacing them as evenly as possible. Use a round-hook serif. Letter widths, pen angles and spacing need to be considered simultaneously. Write the alphabet in sections: A–G, H–N, O–U, V–Z, and repeat each section several times, checking letter proportions and spacing.

CHECKLIST

✔ *Check that pen angles are correct, especially for the steeper strokes of M and N.*

✔ *Note height of crossbars: A and F just below centre. B, E and H just above centre.*

✔ *Join the curves smoothly in C, D, G, O, Q.*

✔ *Align C and G vertically at right, Z at left and right.*

✔ *Be sure V elements of A, M, V, W, X, Y are symmetrical and centred on a vertical axis.*

✔ *Make X and K intersect just above centre, Y at centre.*

✔ *Relate all curves to the circle.*

✔ *Make sure that spacing is even and adequate.*

WORD PRACTICE

Begin writing words as soon as you feel confident with the alphabet, because different letter combinations put spacing to the test. Concentrate on getting a few words right before tackling a longer text. The space between words should be equal and the width of a Roman capital O.

Practise the words shown at right, which contain some tricky letter combinations. Later you can try some words of your own choosing.

1 Write at a letter height of 7 nib widths of a Mitchell No. 1½ nib.

2 Repeat each word several times, checking for letter width, correct pen angle and spacing each time.

3 Use the Rule of Three spacing check (p.25).

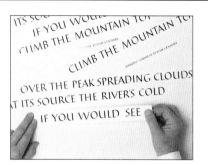

Writing a text in Roman capitals

Even with relatively little experience, you can interpret a simple text in a variety of interesting ways. For this Chinese saying, the text is written in white gouache on grey Ingres paper.

1 *The main text is written using a Mitchell No. 1½ nib. The credit is written with a No. 4 nib. The preliminary version is photocopied and various layout options are tried by cutting and pasting.*

2 *A centred layout is eventually selected for the piece.*

3 *The final version is written in white gouache on grey Ingres paper, on which lines have been lightly ruled.*

The finished piece *Trimmed to the required margins, the completed text makes a simple but effective statement.*

SCALING DOWN

So far you have been practising Roman capitals in a fairly large nib size (Mitchell No. 1½). Smaller nibs are even more demanding on pen control. You can learn such control by working progressively down in size. Keep to one size until you feel confident to move down. The diagram (right) shows sample letters at different nib sizes.

1 *Begin with the largest nib size shown, and write the Roman capitals in their formation groups and/or in alphabetical order. Fine-tune letterforms and spacing as necessary.*

2 *The standard height of 7 nib widths is best for practice in the early stages.*

3 *Repeat this exercise in each nib size, ending with the smallest.*

4 *When writing with very small nibs, keep serifs restrained or they may weaken the letter shapes.*

No. 2 OABCDE

No. 2½ OABCDE

No. 3 OABCDE

No. 3½ OABCDE

No. 4 OABCDE

WRITING LARGE

In some ways, writing with large nibs (greater than Mitchell No. 1½) can be as demanding as writing with small ones. Using an Automatic pen at a height of 7 nib widths means making steady strokes over a long distance. Accurate letter spacing is also more difficult, as you need to stand back to see the spacing clearly. However, large pens offer exciting choices, including double- and multiple-stroke nibs of different widths as well as various sizes of single stroke up to 38 mm (1½").

When writing large, you will need to fill your pen frequently. If direct dipping into ink or paint causes blobby strokes at first, try filling from a large brush (see p. 35). Writing with the grooved side of the nib uppermost usually gives the best ink or paint flow, whereas the grooved side down usually gives sharper edges to strokes. Try your pen both ways, because results vary according to the individual pen and the consistency of the ink or paint. You may have to exert considerable pressure to write sharply with a new Automatic pen. Make sure that no ink or paint dries in the nib after use.

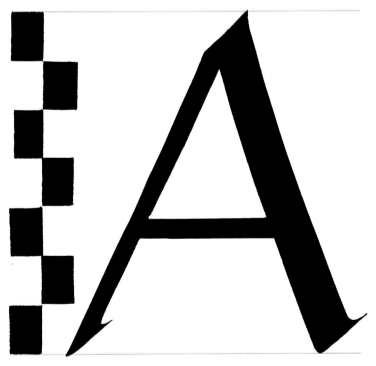

1 *Take a large sheet of layout paper and rule lines 7 nib widths apart. The Roman capital above was written at this height with a 13 mm (½") pen.*

2 *Practise the alphabet, checking the proportions of the letters after each attempt.*

74

Decorated large lettering

Roman capitals written large can be transformed by simple decorative treatment. Here, imaginative use of colour and simple graphic decoration produce bold lettering that serves well as a sign or as part of a poster design. It is written with a 13 mm (¹/₂″) pen in gouache.

1 The first writing of the word in black ink produces some unsatisfactory letter spacing. A photocopy of the lettering is cut and pasted to adjust the spacing.

2 The next stage is to experiment using random letters with different colour changes in the pen (see p. 124) to achieve the desired effect.

3 The first attempt at the final lettering is started, following the pasted-up model and using the selected colour combination.

Finished piece Trials for the decoration using a fine pen are carried out on sample swatches of lettering. The treatment selected consists of fine parallel lines drawn at angles around the letters. The final version shown displays the classic qualities of Roman capitals, softened by the colour selection and subtle decoration.

VARIATION

A freer interpretation of Roman capitals encourages rhythmic writing and may be appropriate to certain texts. However, this should not be tried until you are confident of the principles behind formal Roman capitals and are able to write them accurately.

A slight forward slant, additional rhythm and loosening of the letterforms gives greater movement to the writing. Maintain the letter proportions used for the formal capitals, and minimize the lateral compression that tends to occur when slanting the letters.

ABCDEFG
HIJKLMN
OPQRSTU
VWXYZ

Numerals

MASTERING THE LETTERFORMS

The Romans used letters to write numbers — a system that is still seen in use in certain formal contexts. In the Middle Ages, however, Roman numerals were displaced by the more versatile 10 numeric signs of the Arabic decimal system that we use today. Note the two versions of the number "3", both in common usage.

PI
John Neilson

This dynamic design shows the decorative use of numbers. The numerals are written in contrasting weights and sizes in both ink and gouache.
Dimensions: 40 cm × 27.5 cm (16″ × 11″).

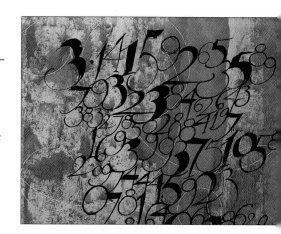

HEIGHT

Ranging numbers are written at the same height as the capitals of the chosen script. With non-ranging numerals, the 1, 2 and 0 are the x height of the script's lowercase letters; the remaining numbers descend and ascend below and above the lowercase x height and are the same height as the capitals.

SLANT AND PEN ANGLE

Numbers can be vertical and based on a circle, or compressed and slanting. However, the numeral 0 is always slightly compressed to distinguish it from a letter O. Compressed and slanting numerals suit a script of similar style, such as italic, but vertical, more circular numbers can also be used with slanting letters. Vertical numbers are written with a pen angle of approximately 30°, and the angle is slightly steepened for compressed numerals. Examples of various styles appear at right.

SPACING

Spacing ("1348", far right) should be generous for the wider, circle-based numbers and slightly closer for compressed numerals. Watch out for uneven or over-close spacing, as this can cause numerals to lose their elegance.

Vertical lined figures

Vertical "Old style"

Slanting lined (compressed)

Slanting "Old style" (compressed)

STYLE

The alignment of numerals in calligraphy depends on the script being used. They can either be aligned at the top and bottom within the letter height (ranging), or written with some above and below the x height (non-ranging). Ranging numbers usually go with capitals for a strong effect. Non-ranging numbers blend with the ascenders and descenders of a lowercase script. The examples shown at right demonstrate the different qualities of the main numeral styles used in different scripts. Note the different spacing requirements of the various examples shown.

14TH AUGUST 1956

Vertical lined figures

14 th August 1956

Vertical "Old style"

14 TH AUGUST 1956

Slanting lined (compressed)

14th August 1956

Slanting "Old style" (compressed)

67890   1348

67890   1348

67890   1348

67890   1348

Formal italic

MASTERING THE LETTERFORMS

With its rhythmic movement and its flowing qualities, italic epitomizes "the dance of the pen". Writing this script on a good surface can be an exhilarating experience. Italic evolved in the early 15th century and owes its name to its Italian origins. Inspired by the Carolingian minuscule scripts of 9th-century France, Renaissance scribes developed a formal script called Humanist bookhand. Seeking a faster style to meet their increasing workload, papal scribes copying documents for the Roman chancery developed the chancery script. More quickly written than the Humanist bookhand, with narrower, forward-slanting letterforms, this script exhibited the flowing qualities characteristic of italic.

In the 16th century a number of writing-instruction manuals were printed from calligraphy cut on wood blocks. The first and most famous was *La Operina* by the Venetian Ludovico Vicentino Arrighi, published in 1522. The manuals show a wealth of italics with many subtle variations. Some have few or no ligatures (connecting lines); others are emphatically cursive (joined and flowing); some have rounded letterforms; others are angular.

MARY MAGDALENE AT THE SEPULCHRE
Joan Pilsbury

This manuscript book written in ink on vellum shows a double-page opening in an elegant formal italic. Dimensions: 32.5 cm × 23.75 cm (13" × 9½").

RENAISSANCE MANUSCRIPT

This fine example of Renaissance italic, with its flowing rhythm, narrow letterforms, sparing flourishes and wide interline spacing, has an elegance that is typical of the best formal italics. The marginal capitals are a type of versal.

However, all exhibit the key features of the italic script: rhythmic, compressed letterforms, springing arches, forward slant, and a relatively steep pen angle of approximately 45°.

Experience with italic handwriting can help promote the fluency needed for all calligraphic work.

The contemporary calligrapher uses two basic italic scripts: formal and cursive. The formal script is an easier one for beginners. A more controlled writing method, it enables the analysis of individual letterforms, providing a sound basis from which to develop the rhythm and flow of the cursive form.

Italic is a versatile script, offering ever more opportunities as you progress. The basic formal and cursive scripts described in this book can be applied in a variety of ways and contexts, as well as providing the basis for many later experiments.

Italic is an excellent script for encouraging rhythm in writing. This is one of the key qualities of calligraphy, and it is important to develop this aspect.

CHARACTERISTICS

Italic is based on the elliptical o, with lateral compression. It has a constant slight forward slant of the downstrokes, and arches that spring from the letter stem.

LETTER HEIGHT
5 nib widths x height. Ascenders and descenders approximately 3½ to 4 nib widths more.

PEN ANGLE
45°.

O FORM
Elliptical, showing the lateral compression characteristic of italic. The o width is about two-thirds of the letter height in skeleton form.

ARCHES
Springing arches also contribute to the flow of the script. They are asymmetrical and start from the letter stem between half and two-thirds up the letter body height.

SERIFS
Simple oval-hook serifs that are integral to the stroke are suitable for a basic italic. Triangular serifs will add a more formal look.

SLANT
Letters may slant forward between 5° and 10° from the vertical, but 5° is sufficient for formal italic.

STROKE ORDER AND DIRECTION
The many upward "push" strokes and few pen lifts help to give italic its flowing quality.

Before writing italic letters with an edged pen, you need to learn the essential skeleton form. Remember that, because italic script consists of compressed forms, all letters (except i, j, m and w) are virtually the same width — many faults in italic are due to incorrect widths. The oval o is shown in a

Skeleton italic

parallelogram with sides slanting 5° from the vertical. The o is a key to letter width, although not to shape; c and e relate to o, but most italic letters relate to the arch shape.

LETTER-FORMATION GROUPS

Italic letterforms are easiest to learn in groups of similar formation, as shown in the geometric diagrams (right).

Clockwise arched letters: h, n, m, r, b, p, k. The group also includes i, which is the beginning stroke of the other letters. The arches spring from half to two-thirds up the x height.

Counter-clockwise arched letters: l, t, u, curved y. Base curves relate to the shape of clockwise arched letters.

Diagonal letters: v, w, x, y, z. The first strokes of v, w, x, y and the third stroke of w must be relatively vertical, so that the axis of the "v" part of the letters has the same slant as the downstrokes of the script.

Oval letters: c, e, o. The c and e are the only italic letters whose shape relates directly to the elliptical o.

Triangular letters: a, d, g, q. These are softened triangles. The curve joins the straight stroke on the right side, half to two-thirds down the x height.

Letters with related top and/or tail curves: f, j, s. The tail curves of f and j mirror the top curve of the f.

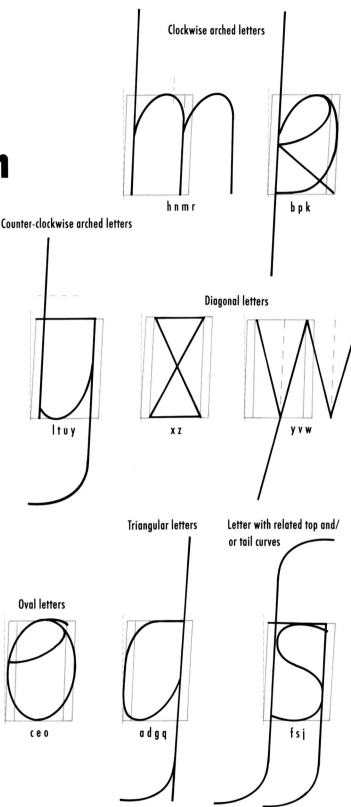

Clockwise arched letters

h n m r   b p k

Counter-clockwise arched letters

l t u y

Diagonal letters

x z   y v w

Oval letters

c e o

Triangular letters

a d g q

Letter with related top and/or tail curves

f s j

SKELETON PRACTICE

Practising in pencil is the simplest way to get the feel of the script and fix the letter shapes firmly in your mind. Spending as much time as you can to acquire accurate information at this stage will make the learning of edged-pen italic easier and more successful.

1 *Rule lines 11 mm (⁷⁄₁₆″) apart.*

2 *With an HB pencil, write the letters in formation groups, working on alternate lines and setting out your work as shown to avoid collision of ascenders and descenders.*

3 *Follow the stroke order and direction shown in the diagrams.*

4 *Aim all straight and curved downstrokes just to the left of six o'clock to give the right amount of forward slant (about 5°).*

5 *Subtly flatten curves such as the sides of a, d, g, q; otherwise they may become too circular.*

6 *Do not lift the pencil off the paper unless indicated by the stroke sequence.*

7 *Draw the letters lightly with the pencil until you begin to feel the form, making alterations along the way as necessary. Write each group several times before moving on to the next.*

SPACING AND WORD PRACTICE

When you feel confident with the letterforms, begin to practise writing words. To do this you will need to consider the letter spacing. Maintain equal space between all letters to achieve a balanced appearance. Try the words shown at right before attempting your own choice of words or a pencil alphabet.

1 *Rule lines 11 mm (⁷⁄₁₆″) apart.*

2 *Write the words in pencil and check the letter spacing according to the Rule of Three (see p. 25).*

3 *When you are satisfied with the individual words, practise writing groups of words, allowing word spaces approximately the width of the o.*

T he versatility of italic makes it an essential part of the contemporary calligrapher's repertoire. Once you are able to write a sound basic italic, you can then create your own variations in letter slant, writing speed, letter width, weight, and other aspects — the possibilities are virtually limitless.

MASTERING THE LETTERFORMS

Weighted italic

The edged pen is a fascinating challenge for calligraphy beginners. Thorough practice of the skeleton letterforms in pencil will have familiarized you with the letterforms and spacing considerations. However, there is one more step that will help you succeed with the pen. Double-pencil italic letterforms will reveal the principle of the two overlapping skeleton shapes that produce the weighted forms.

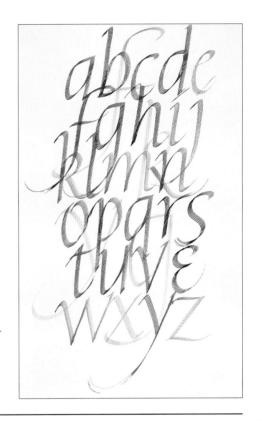

LARGE-SCALE ITALIC

Formal italics written with an edged pen produce lively calligraphic effects.

DOUBLE PENCIL

The two pencil points represent the edge of an edged pen and are aligned at a 45° angle.
1 *Rule lines 32 mm (1¼") apart.*
2 *The points of the pencils should be just under 6 mm (¼") apart.*
3 *Practise writing the letters shown at right. Follow the stroke order and direction you learned for skeleton letters.*

STROKE PRACTICE

As you first practise with the pen, concentrate on achieving uniform thick and thin diagonal and horizontal strokes and straight down-strokes. Practise curved strokes last.
1 *Write between lines ruled at 5 nib widths of a Mitchell No. 2 nib, holding the nib at a constant angle of 45° for all strokes.*
2 *Make sure that the straight downstrokes have a uniform slightly forward slant.*
3 *Variations in stroke width mean that you have changed the pen angle or altered the slant of the strokes.*

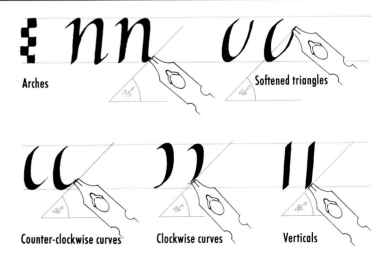

Arches

Softened triangles

Counter-clockwise curves

Clockwise curves

Verticals

ARCHES

Flowing asymmetrical arches are a key characteristic of italic. Creating smooth arches with consistent shapes will help you to achieve a rhythmic, even script. The springing arch leaves the letter stem between half and two-thirds up the x height, and, because the nib is being pushed uphill to the right against its front edge, there is some thickness at the beginning of the springing stroke. It is important to lighten the pressure on the nib on all uphill (push) strokes to enable the nib to move smoothly.

Practising arches will help you acquire the rhythm and flow of italic script.

1 *Rule writing lines at 5 nib widths of a Mitchell No. 2 nib.*
2 *Following the diagram, write a line of repeating i's, n's and m's.*
3 *Re-write the line, alternating the n and m with i. As these are straight-sided letters, they should be easy to space, and this will allow you to concentrate on the arches.*

SERIFS

Oval hooks, which reflect the script's elliptical O, are a good choice for your first italic serif. In formal italic, the serifs are restrained, but a less formal, more rapidly written version will have increasingly pronounced serifs.

When you have mastered the hook serif, vary the effect by adding a sharp-line serif to ascenders and descenders. To achieve a highly formal look, use a built-up triangular serif on ascenders only (see stroke order, far right), ending the descenders with a hook, a sharp line or a slightly uphill light slab.

Hook serif top and bottom

Sharp-line serif top and bottom

Built-up triangular serif top, sharp line bottom

SONNET
Gareth Colgan

This passage from a sonnet by John Donne is taken from a larger work. The quill-written italics rendered in Chinese ink and watercolour on watercolour paper display rhythm and finesse. Dimensions: 60 cm × 25.5 cm (24″ × 11″).

83

LETTER-FORMATION GROUPS

Weighted letters are best learned in groups according to their shape and mode of formation. The groups are the same as for the skeleton forms.

1 Write the groups as shown between lines ruled at an x height of 5 nib widths of a Mitchell No. 2 nib, but leave two x heights clear between each line of writing to accommodate ascenders and descenders.

2 Keep the pen angle at a constant 45°.

3 Practice each group several times, following the model closely. The arrows indicate stroke number, order and direction.

inmhrrbpk

vwxyyz ltuy

ceo adgq ffsj

SPACING EDGED-PEN ITALIC

As italic is a compressed script with letters of *approximately* the same width (excepting m and w), it is more or less equidistantly spaced. Practise the "h i o c" diagram with the edged pen to get the feel of weighted spacing. Remember that curved letters are placed slightly closer than straight letters to create the impression of equal spacing.

hioc

1 Write at 5 nib widths of a Mitchell No. 2 nib, beginning with an h (or an n, if you prefer). Ensure that the letter is the correct width.

2 Write an i next to it, slightly closer than the width of the h counter. Place an o next to the i, fractionally closer still. Write a c alongside the o, even closer but not touching.

3 Re-write the "h i o c" diagram several times.

4 Write out the line n i m i n i m i (p. 83) several times for practice.

Top of crossbar is on or slightly below the line

abcdefghij

Curved and straight strokes join half to two-thirds down the x height

Right and base curves blend

Left and top curves blend

Oval serif

Enclosed top counter is kept above halfway

Tail and straight stroke blend

Tail projects beyond top arm

Two halves are of equal width

Gentle curves

Branch relates to oval o

kklmnopqrs

Rounded counter spacious and oval

Base curve relates to arch shape

Follow-through curve

Top counter minimally smaller — align letter at right with slant of script

Top of crossbar on the line

Keep second stroke straight

tuvwxyz

Maintain forward slant — central axis has same slant as script

Cross minimally above halfway to give balanced letter

Align at right and left with slant of script

The italic alphabet has been labelled with important details to help you write it as accurately as possible. Look at the alphabet as a whole, and take note of these before you begin writing the alphabet.

CHECKLIST

✔ The top of the crossbars of t and f coincide with the top writing line, but can be slightly lower on f.

✔ The s and z align at the right and left with the slant of the script.

✔ The axis of v, x, and diagonal y, as well as the two axes of w, should have the same slant as downstrokes such as i in order to relate them to the slant of the rest of the script. See the v in the alphabet above as an example.

✔ All serifs are smooth, oval and restrained.

✔ The tails of f, g and j have smooth follow-through curves of identical shape.

✔ Check that the top and bottom curves of the o mirror each other.

✔ The curves of b and p are subtly flattened. Base curves should join the stem in a slightly downhill direction to avoid an over-heavy join.

85

JOINS AND ALTERNATIVE LETTERFORMS

Double t, f and ft may be written separately or joined by the horizontal stroke. Double f combinations may consist of two identical f's with extended descenders, joined by their horizontal bar, or a linked combination of two forms (right). Take care when writing r followed by diagonal y: the shape of the y may cause overspacing.

1 *Use lines ruled to 5 nib widths of a Mitchell No. 2.*
2 *Copy the letterforms and combinations shown at right.*

Correct spacing   Incorrect spacing

WORD PRACTICE

As soon as you feel sufficiently familiar with letterforms and spacing patterns, move on to words, which will extend your skills. Continue the practice of writing a word several times and checking the spacing and letterforms each time. Assessing your own writing gives you independence; it means you learn through understanding rather than copying. Although good writing develops gradually with practice, it requires understanding of letterform construction, which comes from adopting a critical approach from the moment that you begin to learn calligraphy.

1 *Write between lines ruled at 5 nib widths of a Mitchell No. 2 nib.*
2 *Repeat each word several times, leaving room for an o between words.*
3 *Correct letters and spacing as necessary.*

lace hall

letter cattle

antirrhinum

Creating texture in colour

Repeated writing of the same word enables you to concentrate on letterforms, spacing and rhythm. At the same time, you can create a close-knit texture on the page, incorporating a subtle range of colours. You can use the same techniques later for exciting work with texts.

For this piece of work, the calligrapher used a Mitchell No. 2 nib and watered-down gouache with colour changes in the pen. An interesting texture and pattern is produced by the graduated colour effect and the pattern of the lettering.

1 Write a word on alternate lines ruled at 5 nib widths of a Mitchell No. 2 nib. At this stage, decisions on the use of colour and an asymmetrical layout have already been made.

2 A review of the first draft shows that standard spacing allows too much white space between the lines, which distracts from the textural effect desired. Your next option is to try closer line spacing.

3 A closer line spacing allows the ascenders and descenders to blend into the adjacent lines of text.

4 The final version can form part of a larger work.

CAPITALS AND WEIGHTED ITALIC

In Renaissance times, plain Roman capitals (p. 64) were commonly used with italic. At line beginnings these were often set with a noticeable gap between capital and following italic minuscule (lowercase) letters. However, a rich variety of flourished italic capitals can also be found in Renaissance manuscripts, and the choice of capitals depends on the context and on the writer's preference. You can use Roman capitals, plain italic capitals (pp. 92–98), or flourished italic capitals (pp. 108–113) alongside italic minuscules.

Plain italic capitals are the easiest to write, although they need accurate letter-width judgement. However, the flowing lines of flourished italic capitals encourage rhythm in writing.

Quotation in italic minuscules

Colour and design are important and rewarding areas to cultivate. Designing a layout for a short text will help you blend good lettering with creative ideas.

Think about the word meanings and jot down any ideas that come to mind about colour, layout and illustration. Satisfactory layout is a matter of individual taste, but there are techniques for achieving the qualities you seek.

1 Use a 20–30 word quotation so that it can be re-written several times if necessary without becoming too trying. Write with a Mitchell No. 2 nib.

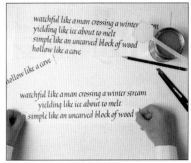

2 Paste up the layout using photocopies. Centre the lines to avoid the square and static look of an aligned block.

3 The finished paste-up acts as a model for the final writing.

4 Try coloured gouache on a word or two. "winter stream" and "ice about to melt" suggest blues and purples.

5 To give the quotation a coloured background, scrape Conté colours with a craft knife and blend the powder on the paper.

6 Gently rub the colour into the paper with a tissue. Spray the background colour with a fixative and dust with gum sandarac.

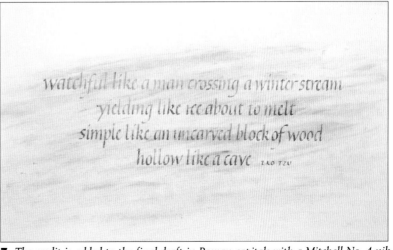

7 The credit is added to the final draft in Roman capitals with a Mitchell No. 4 nib.

WORKING WITH LARGE PENS

Practising any script with large pens loosens writing and encourages rhythm, because the entire arm is used and the rest of the body is more involved. It is also useful for seeing the details of letterforms, such as arch structure, and for studying any letters that seem difficult. The scale enables you to "feel" the letter more as you write, because every slight change of direction is magnified. It is also fun to play with letters and design on a large scale, allowing ideas to flow freely.

1 Write any word at 5 nib widths of a 13 mm (½″) Automatic pen. It is fun to experiment with different pens, but keep an eye on letter proportions or the forms may degenerate.

2 Write in ink or one colour of gouache initially to get used to the pens, then try colour changes in the pens.

3 When you can write the letters accurately, try working more freely and faster, creating texture on the page, or combining lowercase italic with Roman capitals.

Using large pens

Large lettering has many uses — for example, it can be used for headings and as a focal point in a panel of calligraphy. Writing large is a useful skill to master and gives you plenty of scope to be creative. With large lettering, you can really let your imagination run free with innovative uses of colour and layout.

1 A variety of Coit pens is useful for experimentation. Here, several different 13 mm (½″) nibs are tried.

2 The nib selected is used for the whole word, and the colour is changed in the pen (see p. 124). The effect is too static.

3 The word "dance" should really dance. Cut up the lettering and try a layout with some vertical movement to the letters.

4 Move the letters until the right effect is achieved. Paste up the layout and transcribe the finished word.

SCALING DOWN

The smaller the script, the less contrast there is between thick and thin strokes, and therefore great precision is needed when writing with small nibs. As with other scripts, a jump from large to small italic may cause you to lose control of letter shapes, so it is better to work gradually down the nib sizes.

Even if you enjoy writing small, try not to restrict yourself to any particular size, especially at first. The pronounced hand and arm movements needed for larger writing encourage the rhythm and flow that are crucial to calligraphy. Above all, don't work on too small a sheet. Use a sheet of at least 29.5 cm × 42 cm (11″×17″) on a board of 60 cm × 75 cm (24″ × 30″) or larger.

No. 2½

o abcde

No. 3

o abcde

No. 3½

o abcde

No. 4

o abcde

No. 5

o abcde

1 *Rule lines at 5 nib widths of a Mitchell No. 2½ nib, and practise writing the alphabet several times.*

2 *Repeat this exercise in each nib size shown, ruling lines at 5 nib widths of each nib used.*

3 *Check for accuracy of shape and spacing, repeating a size if necessary before moving down. Pay close attention to stroke sharpness and letterforms, which may degenerate at the smaller sizes.*

COMBINING LARGE AND SMALL

Along with good letterforms, spacing and rhythm, it is important to develop a sense of scale by combining different sizes of writing successfully. Combinations are generally used for contrast, but the sizes must harmonize and convey the text appropriately. Sizes should not be too similar, but there are no rules for such decisions: each text needs to be treated according to your own interpretation. A sense of what looks right in terms of text and layout develops with practice and by observing examples of well-designed calligraphy. Analysing the decisions that have been made about scales of writing in the work of other calligraphers is invaluable for your own work.

late summer afternoon, heavy storm breaking light mountain rain, falling veil, fading the land into oblivion

Using large and small italics

Combining large and small lettering is an effective way to add emphasis. When practising, choose a short text so that you can maintain a good standard of writing and spacing. Read the text and decide which words you want to emphasize. In the example, the first two words are selected because they represent a complete thought.

1 Write the quote using a Mitchell No. 4 nib. It is easier to assess where a larger nib may be needed if the whole text is written in the same nib first.

2 Paste up the small lettering using pencil marks on the edge of a separate piece of paper to judge line spacing.

3 Complete the layout. Where line lengths vary, centring the lines is an effective way of adding movement.

4 Write the large lettering in a variety of nib sizes, from Mitchell No. 3½ up to No. 1, on a sheet of layout paper.

5 Try each size. Here, No. 2 is used for the large lettering. Other good contrasts are 1½ and 3½, 2½ and 5, and 1 and 3.

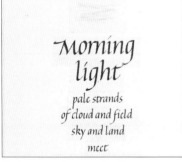

6 Paste up the complete layout, adding flourishes to the last line (see pp. 108-113) to give a softened effect.

7 The illustration was drawn with coloured pencils, crossed by white lines made with an eraser.

Finished piece In the final work, the lettering and the illustration are harmonious.

Italic capitals

MASTERING THE LETTERFORMS

The italic script was used with classical Roman capitals during the Renaissance. These were gradually modified into Humanistic square capitals and flourished italic capitals. Humanistic square capitals remained closely akin to pen-made Roman square capitals. They were often used for text written entirely in capitals, as well as for line beginnings. Flourished italic capitals were a more compressed and slanting form based, like the lowercase script, on the oval O. Inventive and often exuberant, they were used for line beginnings and within italic text. Even among italic capitals, however, Renaissance scribes often retained the wider Roman D.

It is best to learn the compressed italic capitals without flourishes at first, in order to establish accurate letterforms and see the relationships between the letters more clearly. Unadorned italic capitals are useful in their own right, especially for text that is to be conveyed entirely in capitals. They are suitable for formal purposes, such as presentation documents, or for the expressive interpretation of prose and poetry. You will find italic capitals versatile and flowing letterforms that offer many design opportunities.

Once you can write the plain capitals well, it is a relatively simple step to create the flourished versions described on pages 108–113.

THE PLOVER — Louise Donaldson

Written over a wash background, this calligraphic interpretation of a passage from a poem by Robert Louis Stevenson is written in three weights of italic capitals. The larger capitals are written with an Automatic pen with colour change in the pen. The light-weight letters were written with a ruling pen.

JAPANESE POEM
Liz Burch

This delicate panel (left) is rendered in large italic capitals alongside small heavy-weight Roman capitals. Thoughtful placing of rubber-stamp decoration creates a harmonious finished result.

PROSE PANEL
Liz Burch

This panel (right) of strong, well-spaced italic capitals demonstrates that high-quality calligraphy can make an attractive statement without the assistance of additional decoration.

THE GRAND WAY
TO LEARN
IN GARDENING, AS IN
ALL THINGS ELSE
IS TO WISH TO LEARN
AND BE DETERMINED
TO FIND OUT
THE REAL WAY IS TO TRY AND
LEARN A LITTLE FROM
EVERYBODY AND EVERY PLACE

THERE IS NO ROYAL ROAD

IT IS NO USE ASKING ME
OR ANYONE ELSE HOW TO DIG·
I MEAN SITTING INDOORS
& ASKING IT. BETTER
GO AND WATCH A MAN DIGGING
AND THEN TAKE A SPADE
AND TRY TO DO IT
AND GO ON TRYING TILL IT COMES
AND YOU GAIN THE KNACK
THAT IS TO BE LEARNT
WITH ALL TOOLS OF
DOUBLING THE POWER AND
HALVING THE EFFORT

YOU WILL FIND OUT THAT
THERE ARE ALL SORTS OF WAYS
OF LEARNING, NOT ONLY
FROM PEOPLE AND BOOKS BUT
FROM SHEER TRYING

FROM 'WOOD AND GARDEN' BY GERTRUDE JEKYLL

CHARACTERISTICS

Italic capitals are written with the same pen angle throughout. Like italic lowercase, they are based on the oval O and have a constant forward slant.

LETTER HEIGHT	PEN ANGLE	O FORM	SERIFS
8 nib widths.	*45°.*	*The O is oval and in proportion to the lowercase italic o.*	*Oval hooks relating to the oval O for a basic version, but other serifs, such as those described for Roman capitals (p. 65), may be used.*
STROKE ORDER AND DIRECTION *These characteristics are the same as for Roman capitals.*	**SPEED** *Moderate.*	**SLANT** *Approximately 5° forward, as for lowercase italic.*	

93

L ike Roman capitals, italic capitals can be grouped according to their width, although, being more compressed letterforms, the width differences are less marked. However, it is useful to recognize the width differences that do exist before writing out the italic capitals in their weighted form.

Skeleton letterforms

LETTER-FORMATION GROUPS

Italic capitals fall into the same formation groups as Roman capitals, but based on the concept of the oval within the parallelogram instead of the circle within the square. The letters have a 5° forward slant.

Oval letters: O, Q, C, G, D. The C, G and D are seven-eighth-width letters.

Three-quarter-width letters: H, A, V, N, T, U, X, Y, Z. These fit into a parallelogram that is three-quarters the width of the original one. The width has been reduced by one-eighth on each side to give an area approximately equal to that of the oval. The letters in this group are shown in two diagrams for clarity. They are all equal in width at their widest point.

Half-width letters: B, P, R, K, E, F, L, S, I, J. These are about half the width of the original parallelogram, except I and J, which are single-stroke letters. Most of the letters in this group are two-tier letters, based on two ovals inside parallelograms, with the top tier slightly smaller than the bottom in height and width. S aligns at the right with the slight forward slant of the script; it is shown with J, which has the same base curve.

Wide letters: M and W. M fits into the original parallelogram. The central axis of the V part should have the same forward slant as the script. W consists of two V's of equal width, with the same slant.

Oval letters

O   QCGD

Three-quarter-width letters

HAV   NTUXYZ

Half-width letters

BPR   KEFL   SJI

Wide letters

M   W

SKELETON PRACTICE

Practise writing the letters in pencil in their formation groups, paying particular attention to their relative widths. Numerals and arrows show the correct stroke order and direction. Refer to the Watchpoints box on page 98 for additional information on letter construction. Remember to check spacing according to the Rule of Three (p. 25).

1 *Rule double lines 18 mm (³⁄₄″) apart.*

2 *Write the letters in group order, as shown below, using an HB pencil. Follow the stroke order and direction indicated, and write on alternate lines.*

3 *Repeat each group as often as necessary, checking letter widths after each writing.*

4 *Try the alternative stroke order and direction shown for certain letters (see p. 97). Push strokes add continuity to V, W and M, and make a neater follow-through from curve to base in B and D, but they are harder than pull strokes.*

WRITING WORDS

Begin word practice to promote fluency as soon as you feel confident with the italic capitals in alphabetical order.

1 *Write words in pencil between lines ruled at 18 mm (³⁄₄″). Copy letterform and spacing with care.*

2 *Re-write words as often as necessary.*

Once you have mastered the skeleton forms, move on to the weighted versions of italic capitals. As with other scripts, you will find it useful to do some work at the beginning with double pencils, which clearly show the construction of the weighted letterforms. You will also need to give some attention to

Weighted letterforms

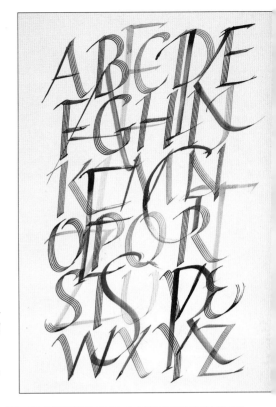

learning the serifs, which are responsible for much of the rhythm and fluidity of this particular script. They help the eye flow naturally from letter to letter along the line. Italic capitals make a very useful script for texts written entirely in capitals where formality is not implied in the words.

ITALIC CAPITALS

13 mm (¹/₂″) single and Coit pens were used with gouache colour changes in the pen for this decorative piece.

PENCIL LETTERFORMS

Your first use of the weighted form could be with either double pencils or a carpenter's (chisel) pencil as shown here. Pay particular attention to stroke joins as you practise.

1 *Sharpen your pencil to a width of 5 mm (³/₁₆″).*

2 *Rule lines 4 cm (1¹/₂″) apart.*

3 *Keep the pencil edge at an angle of 45°, steepening further for the first stroke of M and uprights of N.*

4 *Copy the letters shown at right, referring to the alphabet on p. 98 for additional information if necessary.*

SERIFS

A number of serifs are suitable for use with italic capitals, as shown at right. Oval hooks are the best to try first. They are simple to write and encourage flow and rhythm — unlike built-up serifs, which require pen lifts. Note that the built-up top serifs shown at right are constructed before the downstroke is added. The downstroke thus provides a clean line from top to bottom, as well as completing the serifs.

Oval hook serif   Built-up triangular serif   Built-up slab serif

LETTER-FORMATION GROUPS

Practise weighted letters first in their formation groups to establish accurate letter widths. Look at the alphabet details and checklist on page 98 before writing the formation groups, and check your letter-shapes closely against the examples as you practise.

1 *Write the groups as shown below between lines ruled at 8 nib widths of a Mitchell No. 2 nib.*
2 *Use a pen angle of 45°, steepening to 50°–60° for the first stroke of M and the vertical strokes of N.*
3 *Practise each group several times, following the model closely.*
4 *Check the letters after each attempt, paying close attention to widths.*

SPACING

Establishing the space between the letters in the "H I O C" diagram will guide you towards even spacing with the edged pen. The spacing practised here sets the pattern for all the italic-capital work that follows.

1 *Write the italic-capital H and place an I alongside it at a distance of two-thirds the width of the H counter.*
2 *Place an O slightly closer and a C even closer. Equal spacing requires two straight-sided letters to be furthest apart and two curved letters to be closest together.*

Central axis aligns to forward slant of script

ABCDEF

Curve relates to oval O

Curves enclosing counters relate to oval O

Curves relate to oval O

GHIJKLMN

55°

Curve enclosing counter relates to oval O

Curve enclosing counter relates to oval O

Final stroke almost vertical

Steepened pen angle for verticals

OPQRSTU

Central axis aligns to forward slant of script

Right aligns to forward slant of script

VWXYZ

Right and left align to forward slant of script

Two halves of letter are equal

Diagonals intersect above halfway

The italic-capital alphabet above has been labelled with key points for accurate writing. Take note of these and read the checklist before you begin to write the alphabet. Rule your paper at 8 nib widths of a Mitchell No. 2 nib and write the alphabet in sections: A–F, G–N, O–U, V–Z. Repeat each section several times, checking letter shapes and spacing each time before re-writing.

CHECKLIST

✔ Check that the three-quarter-width letters (H, A, V, N, T, U, X, Y, Z) are equal in width at their widest point, and not wider than O, Q, C, G or D.

✔ Make sure that the pen angle is steep enough for the first strokes of M and N, or the thin strokes will be too heavy.

✔ Letters containing diagonals must have the same 5° slant as the rest of the script — achieved by slanting the V part of the letters.

✔ Maintain the correct forward slant in letters containing diagonals, especially M. Remember that the V part of these letters should have the same slant as the thick downstrokes of the script (i.e., 5°).

✔ Do not allow the final stroke of M to project too far to the right of the vertical, or the letter will look too upright.

WORD PRACTICE

Begin writing these words as soon as you feel confident with the alphabet. Repeating the same few words at first will enhance your accuracy and readiness for unfamiliar letter groupings.

1 *Write at a letter height of 8 nib widths of a Mitchell No. 2 nib.*

2 *Repeat each of the words shown several times, checking letterforms and spacing before re-writing.*

3 *Practise as many times as you need to achieve accuracy and rhythm.*

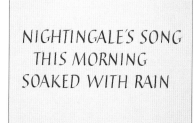

Using italic capitals

Plain italic capitals have a formal feeling, but this effect can be softened with the creative use of colour. Here, the lettering is written over a wash, giving the background the effect of a rainy morning. A Mitchell No. 2 nib is used, and the finished lettering is in gouache.

1 *Write the entire text in ink on layout paper. Cut up the words, finalize the design and then paste up the words.*

2 *Write the quotation on hot-pressed paper using gouache. This leaves a plain white background.*

3 *Alternatively, add a wash to the paper. Once dry, cover with gum sandarac. This will help to sharpen the writing.*

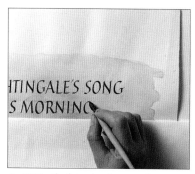

4 *Write the lettering in gouache on top of the prepared wash, again following the original paste-up.*

Finished piece *The result looks formal, but the slight forward slant of the capitals gives a hint of movement, echoing the driving rain.*

SCALING DOWN

It is best to begin learning italic capitals in a large nib size, such as Mitchell No. 1½ or 2, so that all the details of the letters are seen clearly. Once you have achieved accurate lettering and spacing at this size, move down in scale, but do so progressively, adjusting to each size in sequence. The diagram (right) shows some sample letters written in successively smaller nib sizes.

1 *Rule writing lines at 8 widths of the nib you are using.*

2 *Write the alphabet in progressively smaller nib sizes (Mitchell No. 2½, 3, 3½, 4, 5).*

No. 2½   *O A B C D E*

No. 3   *O A B C D E*

No. 3½   *O A B C D E*

No. 4   *O A B C D E*

No. 5   *O A B C D E*

Using italic capitals and lowercase

An interesting contrast can be made by using areas of text written in capital letters alongside those in lowercase. Here, both sets of words are written with a Mitchell No. 4 nib. With capitals, the lettering looks more dominant, lending weight to the words. The words in lowercase have a lighter effect.

1 *Try various designs in pencil thumbnail sketches. This will help you work out which words should be in capitals and which in lowercase.*

2 *Write the words in ink on layout paper, then cut them up for use in making paste-ups.*

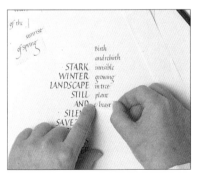

3 *Lay out individual words following the layout of the thumbnail sketch. Select appropriate line breaks and paste up the design.*

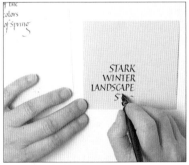

4 *Write the final version of the text following the paste-up.*

Finished piece *Using textured paper for the final piece lends a richer feeling to the work.*

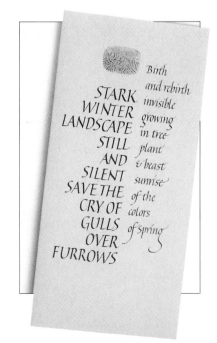

LARGE AND SMALL ITALIC CAPITALS

It is appropriate to write some texts entirely in capitals, and using more than one nib size will give you good practice in balancing different scales of writing. Ensure a standard letter height for each nib size you use, as shown in the example at right. You can also practise varying the standard letter weight to produce either light- or heavy-weight versions of this script with different nib sizes.

MIST·SHROUDED HILLS MUTED COLOURS
STILL AIR OF AUTUMN AFTERNOON COOL AND SILENT· WEAK RAYS OF SUNLIGHT

Using large and small italic capitals

One way to give emphasis to a piece of calligraphy is to use more than one nib size. Some experimentation is required to find suitable contrasts, in this instance, between two sizes of capitals. Here, the small capitals are written using a Mitchell No. 4 nib and the large capitals are written using a Mitchell No. 2½, both at 8 nib widths x height.

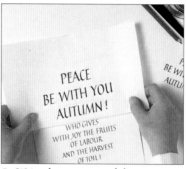

1 *Write the two parts of the quotation in different nib sizes. Select contrasting sizes and paste them up.*

2 *Lay down a background wash on a heavy-weight paper. When this is dry, apply gum sandarac before writing.*

3 *Rule lines over the wash and write the lettering with gum ammoniac, using the paste-up as a guide.*

4 *Apply gold leaf and burnish with a silk cloth. Gently brush off any additional gold.*

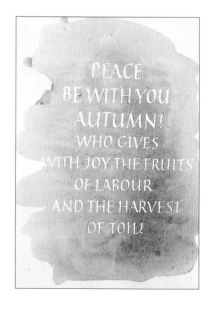

Finished piece *The gold lettering contrasts sharply with the background.*

WRITING LARGE

Large writing calls for sweeping hand and arm movements. It is a pleasure to feel large letters glide swiftly over the page.

1 *Practise a few words with a 7 mm (⁵/₁₆″) Automatic pen.*
2 *Keep the letters well-proportioned at a height of about 8 nib widths.*
3 *Practise first with ruled lines and then try writing freely, judging the height by eye.*
4 *Add colour changes in the pen to vary the effect.*

Using large italic capitals

Large italic capitals can look very attractive. The pen used is a 9 mm (³/₈″) Coit pen that produces just two lines — one thick and one thin. Using a split pen prevents large lettering from becoming too heavy. The space created between the two pen lines adds lightness.

1 *Write the entire text in ink on layout paper. At this stage it is possible to experiment with several Automatic or Coit pens.*

2 *Lay out the words, decide the design and line breaks, then paste up the text.*

3 *Create the background with Conté crayon. Spray with fixative, rule up the paper, and then dust with gum sandarac (see p. 37).*

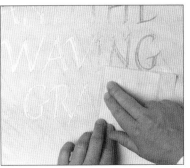

4 *Write the lettering with gum ammoniac. Apply the gold-transfer leaf and burnish with a silk cloth.*

5 *Gently brush off the excess gold to leave the letters sharply distinct.*

Finished piece *The combination of gold lettering over blue and yellow gives an impression of sky and grass.*

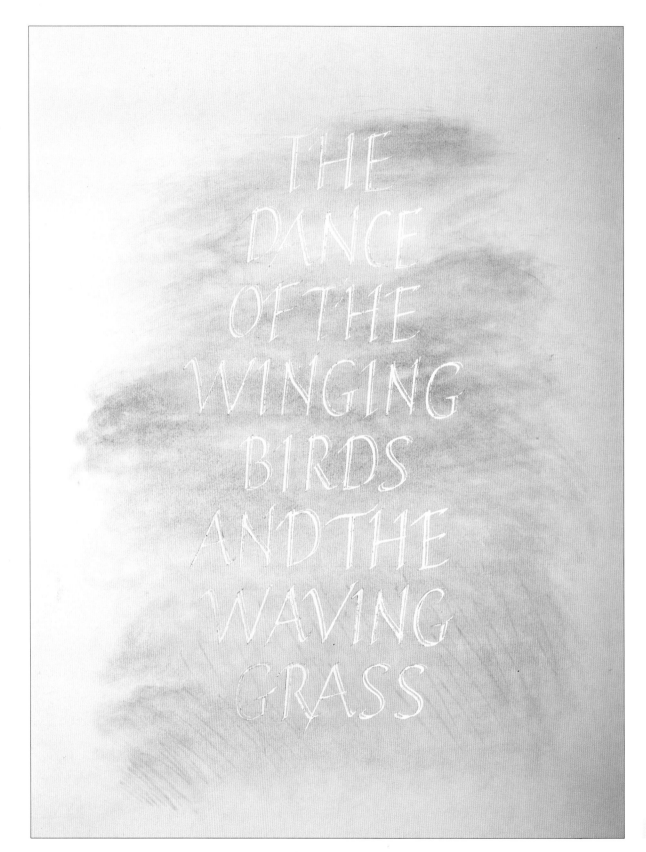

THE
DANCE
OF THE
WINGING
BIRDS
AND THE
WAVING
GRASS

Cursive italic

MASTERING THE LETTERFORMS

Cursive means joined and flowing, and can refer to any script written with few or no pen lifts. The letter joins, known as ligatures, are the product of writing with speed. In italic, they are diagonal or horizontal. The addition of ligatures is an important considera-tion, and in some cases alters the letter con-struction. For these reasons, cursive italic is treated as a separate script.

During the Renaissance many cursive italics were written, each subtly different, depending on the style or choice of the indi-vidual scribe. It is one of the pleasures of cal-ligraphy that each writer can bring a personal interpretation to the most familiar script. It is essential, however, to build such enhance-ments on a thorough knowledge of the basic features of the script.

The rich variety of Renaissance italic conti-nues to provide today's calligraphers with a rich source of reference and experiment. To learn the essential characteristics of cursive italic, you must look at a script as free as pos-sible from personal features. A cursive italic, with the same basic characteristics as formal italic but with the letters linked by ligatures, is the best starting point. For this script you will need to master two key strokes: the thin di-agonal and the weighted horizontal.

TAO TE CHING — Paivi Vesanto

This lively piece of cursive italic shows the use of contrast between narrow and extended letterforms and between heavy- and light-weight characters. The swirling colours of the pastel background add to the movement of the piece. Dimensions: 55 cm × 35 cm (22" × 14").

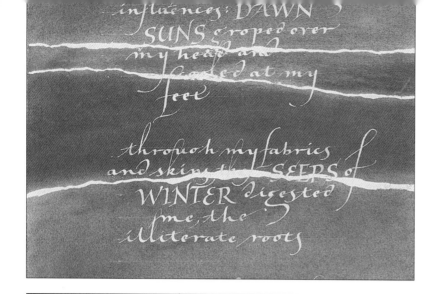

BOG QUEEN – Julia Vance

This detail of a panel of poetry by Seamus Heaney shows a dancing cursive italic with flourishes and subtle italic capitals, written in silver gouache over a pastel background. The thin horizontal lines are gilded. Dimensions 127 cm × 27.5 cm (51″ × 11″).

WEIGHTED HORIZONTAL STROKES

The weighted horizontal stroke is important for the tops of letters such as d, g, q, a, s, f. Some of these letters may start with the top stroke, unlike formal italic. For speed and continuity, the stroke is pushed from right to left. In Renaissance times, these "lids" were often written with a pull from left to right, followed by a push from right to left exactly over the first stroke. This was to avoid lifting the pen off the paper. It is a movement that can still be used in some letter combinations, such as "ma". At word beginnings, however, it is sufficient to start with a right-to-left push stroke. The alternative is to use the formal-italic stroke order (see p. 84). The exercise at right enables you to try three different methods of writing horizontals and to decide which suits you.

1 *Following the example above, try the three methods of writing the letter a.*
2 *Repeat each method of writing several times, and then use each of them in words of your choice.*
3 *You will probably find the first two methods more difficult. These involve push strokes against the front of the nib, but they eliminate pen lifts and ensure writing flow.*

THIN DIAGONAL LIGATURES

The diagonal ligature is a thin uphill push stroke, shown as a broken line joining the serifs in the example at right. It is produced by moving the thin edge of the nib uphill diagonally to the right at a 45° angle. All diagonal joins are parallel.

Following the examples at right, practise the thin diagonals until you have achieved accurate, flowing letterforms.

1 *Rule your lines at 5 nib widths of a Mitchell No. 2 nib.*
2 *Write the letters shown, incorporating thin diagonal joins which are formed by pushing the nib uphill at an angle of 45°.*
3 *Check your writing, making sure that all diagonal joins are parallel.*

USING LETTER JOINS

The various types of joins are shown at right and below.

Diagonal joins (type 1): These occur between letters with a lead-in or lead-out serif. These must be kept thin, straight, and parallel.

Diagonal joins (type 2): These lead from the base of letter bodies.

Horizontal joins: The ligature usually looks less heavy if it is written with a slight curve.

Double letters: These letters can be left unjoined, or joined with preceding diagonal ligatures.

Letters with descenders: Letters ending in a tail to the left are usually unjoined. A join may be added after lifting the pen to give continuity.

acdehi

Diagonal joins (type 1)

klmntu

beps

Diagonal joins (type 2)

forvwx

Horizontal joins

ff tt ff tt

Double letters

gj qyyy

Letters with descenders – unjoined

gy

Letters with descenders –
join after penlift

gy

Letters with descenders –
continuous join

PRACTISING LETTER JOINS

It is a good idea to practise cursive italic first by writing the alphabet with an m between each letter. Use lines ruled at an x height of 5 nib widths of a Mitchell No. 2. (Note: the model below is reduced in size.)

1 *Repeat the alphabet at least twice.*
2 *Check your letterforms, joins and spacing, but concentrate on rhythm.*

ambmcmdmemfmgmhmi

mjmkmlmnmompmqmrm

smtmumvmwmxmymzm

WRITING SMALL

The first exercises for cursive italic use a fairly large nib (Mitchell No. 2), so that details of joins and letterforms can be seen clearly. However, smaller nibs are better adapted to the flow of this script. You may find it easier to develop a rhythm using a smaller nib.

1 *Use a Mitchell No. 4 nib at an x height of 5 nib widths.*
2 *Write the words shown at right in this size.*
3 *Repeat the exercise until you feel at ease with the smaller nib.*

Using cursive script

Although cursive italic is often used for handwriting, it is also suitable for a wide range of calligraphic uses. Here it is used to render a quotation in gouache over a coloured wash. A Mitchell No. 4 nib is used throughout. The cursive hand is written at greater speed than formal italic, the joins drawing the eye naturally from letter to letter.

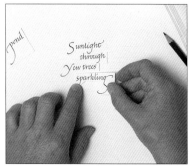

1 Write the text in ink, then cut out and paste up the words. This layout can be copied in gouache for a finished version.

2 An alternative version enlivens the design with flourishes (see pp. 108–113) to some letters in the main text.

3 Cut out and add the trial flourishes to the layout. The exact positioning of flourished ascenders and descenders can be critical.

4 The effect of the layout should be balanced and harmonious.

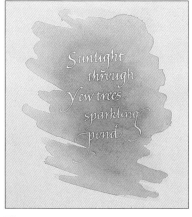

The finished work *uses gold-transfer leaf lettering over a watercolour wash. For further information on applying gold leaf, see p. 101.*

Flourishes & swashes

MASTERING THE LETTERFORMS

The embellishment of letters with ornamental flourishes goes back to the Renaissance. The manuals of the Renaissance writing masters contain a wealth of inventive flourishes. Although the term suggests flamboyance, flourishes can range from subtle stroke extensions to elaborate traceries of loops and lines. They can be a wonderful enhancement to calligraphic work, provided they are carefully matched to their context. Sign-writing, commemorative inscriptions, diplomas, greetings cards and personal work are just some of the areas in which they can be used with a restrained or spirited effect.

Flourishes must appear to be an intrinsic part of the letter, not a contrived addition. They need to be written with flowing movement, speed, directness — and good pen control. In the enthusiasm for writing flourishes, it is easy to neglect the letter shapes themselves. These must be accurate if letter and flourish are to form a harmonious whole.

Some people take rapidly to writing flourishes, but whether you find flourishes easy or not, it helps first to understand the principles of good flourish design. Remember that the choice of flourish depends on the design context and the purpose of the calligraphy. Begin by learning some basic flourish shapes, but also study the creative ideas of other calligraphers, past and present. Look for inspiration in the imaginative flourishes of such Renaissance calligraphers as Arrighi, Tagliente and Palatino, which you can find in illustrated books, and in the work of accomplished 20th-century calligraphers, who have developed innovative lettering for contemporary needs.

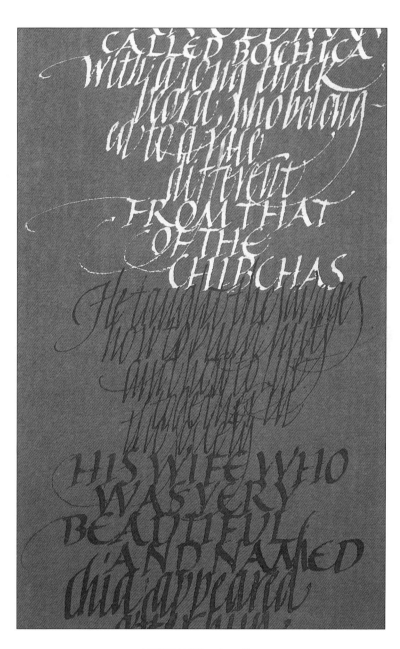

POETRY PANEL — Paivi Vesanto

Elegant flourishes form a natural part of these freely written italics and italic capitals.

FLOURISHED CAPITALS

Because of their role in titles and at text beginnings, capitals are usually the first letterforms to be considered when learning flourish design.

You can add flourishes to the entire capital alphabet with the aid of four basic flourish types. These are shown below. Each flourish is complete. Each group begins with a simple flourish and progresses to more complex variations. Acquire a basic repertoire of flourishes by practicing the direction groups below.

1 Rule lines 7 mm ($^1/_4$") apart, the equivalent of 8 nib widths of a Mitchell No. 4 nib.
2 Use a pencil at first, so that your hand and arm are not restrained by the resistance of the broad nib against the paper. With practice, this resistance should not be a problem.
3 Loosen up with some large, sweeping movements, such as the tail on the R. Let the pencil move lightly over the paper.
4 Copy flourishes from each group, in the order shown, until you have memorized them well enough to write without hesitation.
5 When you feel confident with your pencil, repeat the exercise with a No. 4 nib.
6 You may need to make several attempts at each flourish to produce flowing lines.

Lead-in flourishes

Flourishes aligned to slant of script

Extended diagonals to right

Extended diagonals to left

SWASH CAPITALS

Swash capitals are relatively simple flourished letters that are ideally suited to line beginnings — for instance, in poetry. Swash capitals also make an excellent script for use in posters and other display work. The alphabet at right provides a good starting point for beginners. To write these letters with both flow and control, copy the alphabet, following the stroke order and direction indicated.

1 *Rule lines to a height of 8 nib widths of a Mitchell's No. 2 nib.*

2 *Practise the capitals in alphabetical order, writing each letter several times before moving on to the next letter.*

3 *Take care with letter spacing, so that swashes do not overlap.*

4 *When you have gained in confidence, try some swash capitals in a text of your choice.*

FLOURISHES FOR LOWERCASE ITALIC

Flourish design for lowercase italic follows the same principles as for capitals. There are two main directions in which the flourish can travel. At right you will find examples for y and h, moving from a simple flourish to more complex designs.

Practise flourishes for italic minuscules with the designs for y and h shown.

1 *Rule lines 5 mm (³/₁₆″) apart, the correct x height for a Mitchell No. 4 nib.*

2 *Practise each letter several times in pencil until you are familiar with the design.*

3 *Repeat the exercise using a Mitchell No. 4 nib, omitting any flourishes that are too difficult at first.*

4 *Make sure that the reservoir moves easily up and down the nib, or the ink flow will be restricted and the pen will not move easily over the paper.*

D E F F G H

K L L M N N

Q R S T U V

W X Y Y Z

h h h h h h h h h h h

y y y y y y y y

EXPERIMENTING WITH FLOURISH DESIGN

Once you are familiar with some basic flourishes, try making your own designs. Planning in pencil or felt-tip pen will enable you to work faster and more freely.

1 *Write spontaneously, letting the ideas flow.*

2 *Follow up with design refinements using the edged pen.*

FLOURISH EXPERIMENT

In this decorative piece of work, carefully planned flourishes connect the spaces and carry the eye into the design.

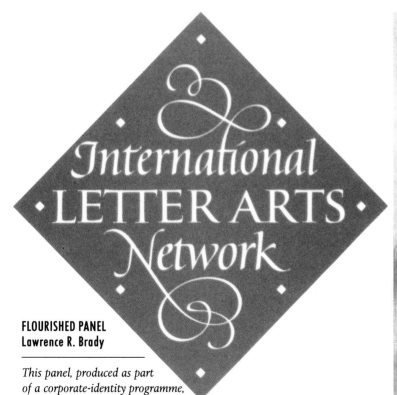

FLOURISHED PANEL
Lawrence R. Brady

This panel, produced as part of a corporate-identity programme, uses carefully considered flourishes at the top and bottom. These flowing strokes help to integrate the different elements in the design.

CHECKLIST FOR IMPROVISED FLOURISHES

✔ *Spontaneous flourishes depend on knowledge and pen control.*

✔ *Write flourishes smoothly and rhythmically. Speed develops with practice.*

✔ *Write flourishes continuously. It is necessary to break them into component strokes only when writing with a very large nib, and not always then.*

✔ *Where straight lines and curves join, make sure the transition follows through in a fluid movement.*

✔ *Establish a sense of spaciousness around the letter. Over-close flourishes create a cramped design.*

✔ *Diagonal strokes are usually parallel. Do not write them too close together, or the flourish will look heavy.*

✔ *Design and practise flourishes in pencil for uninhibited movement and speed.*

✔ *Practise with chisel-edged brushes or large chisel-edged felt-tip markers to loosen arm movement and encourage experimentation.*

Using flourishes

Flourishes should be carefully proportioned and must relate to, and not obscure, other parts of the text. For a certificate, poster, title page or dust jacket such as the one shown here, a decorative flourished heading or other flourished design element may be useful. There is more scope for flourishing if there is adequate surrounding space.

1 *Much of the success of flourishing comes from detailed planning of the design. Here preliminary pencil roughs are sketched.*

2 *When first learning to design flourishes, it may help to pencil the flourishes on to the simple letterforms written in ink.*

3 *Several different flourish designs are written using a Mitchell No. 2 nib. Each design is then considered within the context.*

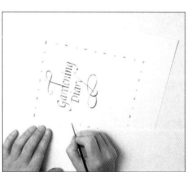

4 *The final design is written in gouache, and a decorative border is added in gouache with a brush.*

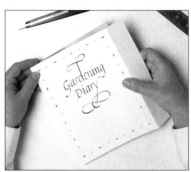

5 *The paper is then trimmed to the dimensions of the book, leaving a flap 2.5 cm (1") wide on each end that folds inside the cover.*

AMPERSANDS

Symbols other than standard letterforms may also be flourished or written in unusual ways. An example is the sign for "and" known as an ampersand. An ampersand must harmonize with the script being written, and a simple design may suit the context better than a flamboyant one. Three examples of ampersands suitable for use with contemporary calligraphy are shown at right, together with the stroke sequences for writing them.

1 *Rule lines to a height of 8 nib widths of a Mitchell No. 2 nib.*

2 *Practise each of the ampersands in turn, first on their own and then in context with an appropriate script.*

Type 1

Type 2   Type 3

Versals

Versals are capitals, built up with pen-made compound strokes. In medieval times they were used to draw the reader's eye to headings, important sections of text or verse beginnings. The finest examples of pure versal letterforms are from the Carolingian period of the 9th and 10th centuries. These graceful letterforms reflect the proportions of the Roman inscriptional capitals on which they were based.

Today, versals are useful for titles and for interpretive work with prose and poetry. They can be used in their classical forms, or with variations in height, weight, slant or letter width that give scope for exploration.

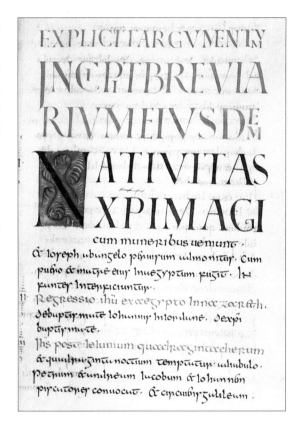

MEDIEVAL MANUSCRIPT

This early medieval manuscript shows the traditional use of versals for introductory text and for illuminated letters.

CONSTRUCTION

Versals are built stroke by stroke using a technique that is close to drawing. The thick compound strokes, which are a major feature, consist of two slightly curved outer strokes, filled with a final single stroke.

As their shapes are based on Roman capitals, the best preparation for learning versals is to practise skeleton Roman capitals in pencil, as shown on page 67, at a height of 2 cm ($\frac{3}{4}$"). Then try the basic component strokes shown below and on the facing page: thick verticals, thick diagonals, thin diagonals, curves, thin verticals and thin horizontals. Practise each stroke with a Mitchell No. 4 nib on lines ruled at 24 nib widths. Then try the sample letter that incorporates that stroke.

Thin verticals

1 *Hold the nib edge at a 0° pen angle and draw a horizontal top serif.*
2 *Maintaining the same pen angle, draw a vertical downstroke.*
3 *Add a shaping stroke and horizontal serif at termination.*

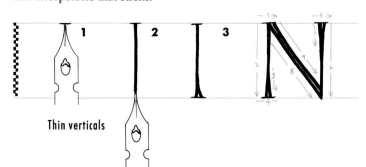

Thin verticals

Thick verticals

1 *Draw a horizontal top serif as before.*
2 *Maintaining the same pen angle of 0°, draw the left downstroke with a slight inward curve.*
3 *Leave a gap of 1 nib width, and draw the right downstroke, also curving inward. The form should be heaviest at the top.*
4 *Place the nib at the top of the gap and pull the ink down to fill the gap. Finish with a horizontal stroke, completing the bottom serif.*

Thin diagonals

1 *Draw a horizontal top serif as before.*
2 *With the nib at 90° to the stroke direction, draw a downward diagonal.*
3 *Finish with a shaping stroke and a horizontal serif.*

Thick diagonals

1 *Draw a horizontal top serif as before.*
2 *With the nib at 90° to the stroke direction, draw the left downward diagonal.*
3 *Continue as for thick verticals (above).*

Horizontal arms

1 *Hold the nib edge at 90° to the horizontal, and pull it to the right.*
2 *Add flaring with a shaping stroke between the main stroke and the serif.*
3 *Maintaining the 90° pen angle, add a vertical serif at termination.*

Curves

1 *Start with a pen angle of about 15° to the horizontal to give slight weight to the thinnest parts of the curved letters, at top and bottom. Draw the inside curve first.*
2 *Add the outside curve with a 0° pen angle. The distance between the two curves should be 1 nib width at its widest point — half way up the letter height.*
3 *Fill the gap with a third stroke.*

SPACING

Versals are elegant letters which require generous, accurate spacing. Over-close or erratic spacing destroys the effect. Use the "H I O C" diagram (right) to establish the correct spacing pattern before practicing the alphabet. Practise the diagram, checking the spacing by eye.

Thick verticals

Thin diagonals

Thick diagonals

Horizontal arms

Curves

Circular outer curves

Added stroke for shape

Oval bottom counter

Gradual transition from straight to curved strokes

Added stroke at termination

Added strokes to horizontal

Aligned at right, serif below halfway up the letter height

Horizontal just over halfway up letter height

Slight thinning at mid-point

Gradual transition from straight to curved strokes

Vertical letter with equal-width counters

Added strokes for shaping

Vertical axis

Curve meets stem halfway up the letter height

Bowl joins horizontal nearly halfway down the letter height

Circular counters

Aligned vertically at left and right

Gradual transition from thick vertical to curve

Slight thinning at centre of thick diagonals

Crosses slightly above halfway up the letter height

Diagonals meet halfway down the letter height

After practising the components of versals and the "H I O C" spacing diagram, try writing the alphabet. The component strokes of versal letters are assembled in the same order as the individual strokes of Roman capitals (see p. 66).

CHECKLIST

✔ Make sure that all thick verticals and diagonals measure 3 nib widths.

✔ Base your letter proportions on skeleton Roman capitals (p.66).

✔ Thick components should not be heavy or over-shaped. The first two strokes should be almost parallel with minimal inward curving.

✔ Hold the nib at 90° to make horizontals 1 nib width wide. Left-handers will probably need to hold the nib at about 45°, widening the stroke with an additional stroke.

✔ Do not over-state the flaring at the open ends of thin strokes.

✔ Check that serifs are fine, and not too long.

✔ Make sure that the outside of a curved letter is round.

✔ Check that the fullest point of a curve equals or slightly exceeds the width of a thick stem.

Using versals

Although versals are formal, they can be used in many creative ways. This example, written in white gouache on a coloured paper or background, is particularly delicate.

1 *First write the full text in versals in black ink on layout paper. Here a Mitchell No. 4 nib is used.*

2 *Cut and paste the text. Try various layouts before deciding on a design.*

3 *Prepare the colour washes, blend the colours and try them on the same kind of paper to be used for the final work.*

4 *When you are satisfied with the colours, apply the wash.*

5 *When the wash is completely dry, rule the paper following the selected layout. Prepare the surface with gum sandarac (see p. 37).*

6 *Write the text in white gouache over the wash. Load the paint into the pen using a brush.*

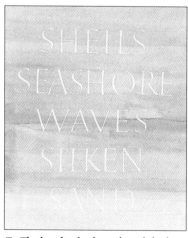

7 *The bands of coloured wash look like sand, sea and sky, reflecting the text.*

8 *An alternative finished version uses lettering written with gum ammoniac and gilded.*

4

Colour and image

What is colour?

COLOUR AND IMAGE

Darkly inked letters on a white page, with their balance of contrast, shape and texture, can be the perfect choice for a piece of work. As traditional scribes knew, however, the use of colour can add character and substance, and widen the opportunity for self-expression. In creative work especially, colour, word and image can work together to convey a theme, express a mood, emphasize an interesting surface, or explore an idea. Colour may come from paper, ink, paint, coloured pencil, pastel or other materials. It may be applied to a single letter, to a border, or over an entire design. It may be restrained or elaborate, a subtle background, a glimmering highlight, or a joyous outpouring. Its appropriateness and success will depend on your knowledge of the materials and understanding of how to combine them with text, script and layout.

ASPECTS OF COLOUR

When working with colour, it is important to be aware of the different qualities of the colours we see and how these qualities can be incorporated into a work of calligraphy by the use of different colour media. Our appreciation of colour is governed by the eye's reaction to light of different wavelengths, enabling us to distinguish between the colours of the spectrum — red, orange, yellow, green, blue, indigo and violet. The vast range of colours that our eyes can register is produced by different mixtures of these wavelengths. Similarly, the pigments used in paints can be mixed in different ways to produce colours with precise characteristics. On the following pages examples of colours in nature are shown alongside painted examples to demonstrate sources of inspiration for colour choices in your calligraphy.

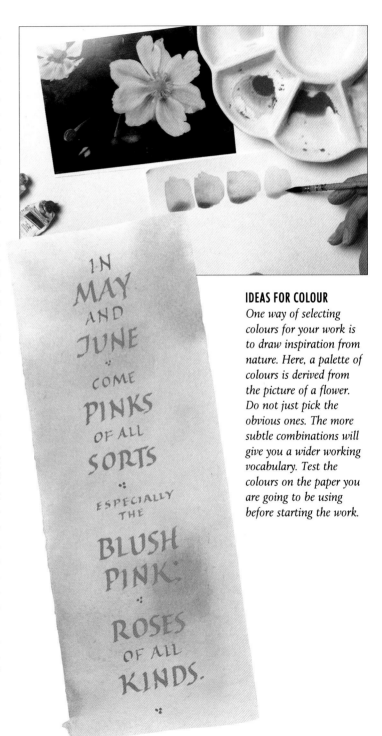

IDEAS FOR COLOUR
One way of selecting colours for your work is to draw inspiration from nature. Here, a palette of colours is derived from the picture of a flower. Do not just pick the obvious ones. The more subtle combinations will give you a wider working vocabulary. Test the colours on the paper you are going to be using before starting the work.

THE COLOUR WHEEL

Exciting colours can be found in tubes or pans, but by mixing colours yourself you can greatly increase your options. A useful basis for experimentation is the colour circle, or wheel, which provides a structured guide to the functions and relationships of colour (below).

Red, yellow and blue are the primary or basic) colours from which others can be derived. The secondary colours are those produced by mixing the primary colours: orange (from red and yellow), green (from yellow and blue), violet (from blue and red). A mixture of all three primary colours makes grey. The tertiary colours are created by mixing equal proportions of a primary colour and its adjacent secondary on the colour wheel. Three primaries therefore produce three secondaries, and these together produce six tertiaries, giving a colour wheel of a dozen hues.

Careful control over the proportions of each colour used is important both to achieve a successful result and to be able to repeat it. It also helps to give you clear colour ideas when planning a design. Making your own colour wheel will give you the basic knowledge you need to mix colours successfully. You can also practise controlling proportions by choosing two primaries and mixing them to make a colour scale that moves in graduated steps from one colour to another — for example, from blue through purple to red. Keep notes and examples of various mixtures.

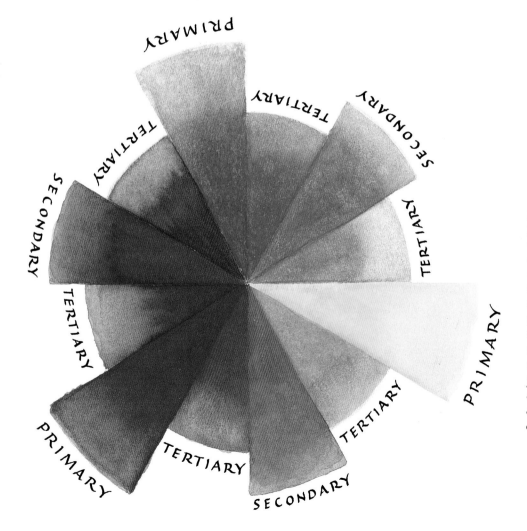

MAKING YOUR OWN COLOUR WHEEL

Investigate the colour possibilities of three primary colours by making your own colour wheel. In addition to creating nine additional colours from the three primaries, within each segment you can achieve further variations by using paint at different dilutions, producing different degrees of opacity.

VALUE

Each basic colour (or hue) has either light or dark value. For example, yellows have a lighter value than blues. The value of a particular colour can generally be lightened by dilution and darkened by being mixed in a higher concentration.

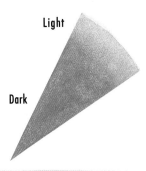

Light

Dark

COLOUR TEMPERATURE

Colour temperature helps to create mood, space and the appearance of modelling. Warm colours seem to advance, and cool colours to recede. Colors are categorized as warm by association with the sun or fire, and this quality is evoked by rich yellows, reds and colours adjacent to these. Cool colours are associated with ice, water and sky, and include shades of blue, violet and some greens.

Most colours can be made warmer or cooler by adding warm or cool pigments, red-orange being the exception. Placing cooler colours beside warmer ones heightens the sense of coolness or warmth.

Warm colours

Cool colours

COMPLEMENTARY COLOURS

These are positioned directly opposite each other on the colour wheel. Mixed in equal quantities, they neutralize each other. A small quantity of colour has a slightly dulling effect when added to its complement. The juxtaposition of complementaries creates vibration, which is why orange letters on blue do not read easily.

Complementary colours

ANALOGOUS COLOURS

These are colours adjacent to each other on the colour wheel — yellow, yellow-green and green, for example. They are used to create mood and temperature and to enhance harmony.

Analogous colours

BUYING PAINT

The first colours you will need to buy are the three primaries in either gouache or water-colour. There are many brands and blends of red, yellow and blue, and each of these will produce a different hue. This is because primary pigments have a natural (or manufactured) bias toward one of the secondary colours. For example, ultramarine blue has a tendency towards violet, and cerulean blue toward green; cadmium red is a red-orange, and alizarin crimson has a violet tinge, cadmium yellow has an orange hue, and lemon yellow is slightly green. This colour bias will affect your attempts to mix a "pure" range of secondaries and tertiaries. When making your first colour wheel, you should look for middle-range primaries with the least tendency toward the secondary colours of orange, violet or green.

For a basic palette, it is advisable to have two reds, two blues and two yellows, each containing an opposite colour bias. This will give you a varied and reliable working range of pigments. Remember that watercolour produces a more transparent colour than gouache. The choice of paint type will therefore depend on the effect you want.

Cadmium yellow

Lemon yellow

Cadmium red

Alizarin crimson

Ultramarine blue

Cerulean blue

KEEPING COLOUR NOTES

It is a good idea to keep a folder of colour examples and notes on how you mixed them. These will be your reference for subsequent matching and planning, helping you to visualize similar or alternative colour choices and stimulating new ideas. Use the folder, too, for photographs or clippings showing colours or colour combinations that appeal to you, as well as pieces of material, leaves, paper wrappers, labels or any other item whose colours catch your eye and which you might use for inspiration.

Using colour

COLOUR AND IMAGE

A textured effect or a wash of a unified tone can be applied to the paper to give a coloured background for calligraphy. However, adding this colour involves water, which may cause the fibres in the paper to swell and the sheet to wrinkle as it dries. The larger the surface, the more prone it will be to wrinkling. One way to avoid wrinkling is to use a heavy paper. A weight of 140 lb or so is suitable for most purposes, but, if a large amount of water is used, a 200-lb or 300-lb

paper may be needed. Lighter papers will resist wrinkling if they are stretched before use (see instructions on the facing page).

A background built with individual brush-strokes separately applied will show streaks and variations of colour where the paint over-laps and dries irregularly. This method could be used to create texture. More often, how-ever, you will want the subtler all-over effect achieved by "laying a wash". Methods for applying and blending washes are shown on the following pages.

Once you have developed the skill of laying a wash, you can achieve many exciting variations and textures. There is just one cau-tion: bear in mind that you are going to write on the surface. If the background paint is too thick, paint from the pen will spread into it, blurring the writing, or you may be unable to write properly at all, so keep the paint thin under the area in which you intend to write.

DETAIL BRUSHES
Should be springy red sable with well-pointed tips.

WASH BRUSHES
Can be round or flat. They should be soft and capable of holding plenty of water.

COLOUR IN THE PEN

A single colour in the pen may be transparent or opaque. By starting with one colour in the pen and gradually introducing a second colour as you re-load the pen, you can create an interesting graduated effect. The pen can also create a broken succession of marks that contrast with areas of solid colour in background washes. You could create tonal changes: light to dark or dark to light, or repeated sequences of light and dark. Variations can be introduced through different nib sizes or textural effects.

Papers that are to receive a watercolour background may need to be stretched before use to prevent them from wrinkling. For this you will need a rigid board (such as a drawing board) larger than the sheet to be stretched, and some gummed brown-paper tape.

1 Check the paper against the board to make sure that it does not overlap. There should be at least 4 cm (1½″) leeway on all sides. Choose which side of the paper is to be the work surface.

2 Immerse the paper in cold water in a sink or other suitably sized container for a minute or two. Alternatively, wet the paper under cold running water.

3 Lift the paper carefully and allow the excess water to drain from one corner. Take care not to rub water across the surface of the wet paper, as this may damage the fibres, causing uneven paint effects.

4 Lay the paper on the board gently. Cut eight strips of gummed tape slightly longer than the sides of the sheet — two for each side. Wet the tape with a sponge.

5 Apply a tape strip along each edge of the paper so that it overlaps by about 6 mm (¼″). Smooth it down to attach it to the board. Repeat with the remaining strips. Set the board aside to dry, flat and away from any heat source.

LAYING A WASH

1 Use stretched paper still attached to the board. Work with the board slightly tilted. Load a thick, flat brush with paint and apply horizontal strokes across the board. Allow each brushstroke to overlap the last.

2 Continue to work down the paper, re-loading the brush at the end of a stroke, not halfway through. Keep the strokes smooth and even. Do not try to re-work a stroke that may not be perfect — this is liable to make matters worse.

3 When you finish laying the flat wash, the overlaps should gently blend together, leaving a flat field of background colour.

BLENDING TWO COLOURS

1 Apply two colours — one from the top, the other from the bottom — on the stretched paper as if they were flat washes (see p. 125). The paper and board should be flat. It may help to wet the paper first.

2 The amount of overlap between the two colours can vary along the join. Let them bleed into each other.

3 The crossover of colour can be controlled by tipping the board, first in one direction, then in another.

BLENDING SEVERAL COLOURS

1 Try applying several washes to the stretched paper with a wide brush.

2 You do not have to lay the colours in simple strips — they can bleed and overlap freely.

3 To bleed the colours, tilt the paper and board until the colours run into one another.

WET INTO WET

1 For an effective way of making a mood-evoking background that does not distract from the calligraphy, apply areas of gouache over a wash that is still wet.

2 The wet gouache bleeds into the background wash, blurring the edges and creating a soft, blended effect.

3 By dabbing the surface with tissue paper, it is possible to control the bleed and therefore to determine the finished effect.

MULTI-COLOUR SPATTER

1 For another way of producing an interesting background colour, try spattering the stretched paper with paint.

2 Use a stencil brush that is loaded with paint, and flick it with the tip of your thumb. You can use more than one colour.

3 Remember to wear old clothes when you do this, as spots of colour fly everywhere. Limit the number of colours you use in any one area, or the result will look muddy.

MASKING-FLUID RESIST

1 Apply masking fluid to stretched paper with a paintbrush. Rub off any unwanted fluid with your finger.

2 When the masking fluid is dry, lay your coloured washes over it.

3 Once the colour is dry, rub away the masking fluid with your finger, exposing the white of the paper.

ALTERNATIVE MATERIALS

Backgrounds treated with coloured pencils, watercolour pencils or pastels make interesting alternatives to coloured paper or paint.

Coloured pencils should be used with minimal pressure. To strengthen the tone, build up layers of light strokes, one on top of the other, or use cross-hatching.

Watercolour pencils are available in hard or soft grades and should be chosen to match your paper. A soft pencil is suitable for a soft paper, whose fibres could be torn by a hard point. A good way to use watercolour pencils is to work the colour on to your paper from the pencils and then brush water over the coloured surface. Conté crayons and those made from dry pigment and gum tragacanth or similar mixtures also produce exciting background effects.

Conté crayons

Watercolour pencils

Coloured pencils

Interpreting the text

4 COLOUR AND IMAGE

The mood and meaning of the text you are writing will suggest the choice of colour, design and letterform. Aspects to consider include the sense and inflection of the words, associated connotations and the use of contrasts. These have parallels in colour terms. Tonal changes and use of the analogous range (p. 122) — for example, moving progressively from blue to green — create colour harmony. This is also a good method of invoking mood and warmth or coolness.

Explore colour considerations during the layout stage of a design (p. 48). Paint your colour choices on tracing paper, which you can place over the layout and adjust as necessary.

It is wise to keep your colours understated at first and to work from light to dark. Colour immediately attracts the eye, and bright colours will appear to come forward off the page. This can be helpful in enlivening a design or adding judiciously chosen emphasis. The eye's unconscious tendency to travel around a layout, linking like colours, can also be used to create unity. But colour can easily be over-done, and it should therefore be approached with caution.

Visualizing colour as mass and the lines of text as strands to be linked compatibly with it can help you to assess suitable contrasts. For example, if the text suggests liveliness and activity, contrast this with a calmer background to avoid a muddled effect.

Elements such as verticals and horizontals can also create contrasts and tensions. A design can be strengthened by emphasizing these. The text itself, being a linear form, may be written vertically or horizontally, or compressed and angled to intensify tensions. To relax this tension, spread the verticals or horizontals further apart.

CONTROLLING COLOUR

One rough idea for this quote suggests winter colours giving way to warmer tones (top). Another shows the lifting of winter gloom (middle). A third moves from winter to spring in a monochromatic progression (above).

SOURCES OF INSPIRATION

Ideas for the dynamics of design — structure, layout, colour, pattern, texture, rhythm and mood — are most readily found in the environment. Look keenly at the world around you, analysing it in visual terms and training your eye to seek out patterns, harmonies and juxtapositions of texture, line and colour. Here, a starfish, grass shoots, thorns and woven rushes illustrate contrasting design possibilities. Practise interpreting what you see in terms of colour and design. Record your observations in notes, sketches or photographs, putting together a valuable source of stimulation for design ideas.

COLOUR AND DESIGN

The design for a piece of coloured calligraphy should be started with a number of thumbnail sketches.

1 The quote mentions leaping, which suggests a vertical design.

2 However, trout do not leap in a regular fashion, so an asymmetrical design is tried.

3 In fact, a combined vertical and horizontal layout for the river works better.

4 The design is refined, and the colour of the background is developed. The finished work combines the splash of the leaping trout with the peaceful colours of woodland and water.

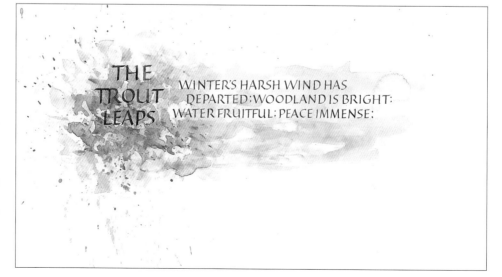

THE TROUT LEAPS

WINTER'S HARSH WIND HAS DEPARTED: WOODLAND IS BRIGHT: WATER FRUITFUL: PEACE IMMENSE:

WORDS AND ILLUSTRATION

Whether you use colour or not, any image you choose should augment the meaning of the words. Text and image should be visually harmonious. Decisions on how to blend the two take place when you make thumbnail sketches or at the layout stage.

It is important to consider the overall space in which image and text appear, and not to use decorative letters or illustrations merely as space fillers. The "negative" areas — those which are left free — are as essential to balanced layout as the positive ones. It is the shapes of spaces and marks together that make up the design. An image or illustration also contains negative areas, and these should be given equal consideration.

CHOOSING A FOCAL POINT

Begin by choosing a focal point: the part of your layout to which the eye will be guided first. You could feature this as a larger, darker, lighter or more colourful letter, word or image. You could establish an "active" area in which greater numbers of shapes or letters are closely gathered. Or you could draw, write or paint an especially vigorous textural or visual element.

It is usually best to work from the focal point, so that no other text or image competes with it. If you establish two equally active areas, for example, the eye will look from one to the other, separating the design into rival parts. This does not mean that you cannot use another focal point, but that the second one should be more muted and should enhance the strength and direction of the main focus.

The position of the focal point needs to be carefully chosen. In the exact centre of the design, it may look too obvious and therefore uninteresting. Too near the edge of the page, it may seem about to slip off. If it links too powerfully with another part of the design, it may divide the paper. In the same way, the text and the image should not divide the surface equally. If each occupies half the sheet, for example, the design is likely to be monotonous. Using too many colours steals attention from the image and the words. Intense colour should not be used on insignificant detail.

There can be many sources of ideas for calligraphic composition and illustration. Get into the habit of looking at the environment around you and taking notes on interesting colours, textures and objects that could be used in your work. Keep a scrapbook of these notes. Sketch in ideas for layouts, paste in photographs you find interesting, and use these for colour and letterform observations.

SEEING NEGATIVE SHAPES

Try to see each of your layouts in terms of the negative areas that it creates. These shapes are an essential part of the design. The layouts shown at left are shaded to draw your attention to the negative areas that they create.

If you decide to fill a negative area with an illustration, be sure to check that this does not alter the balance of the design.

DETERMINING THE FOCAL POINT

The focal point is the point of the image to which the eye is first drawn. Here, the left-of-centre focal point is determined by the area of darkest colour in the background wash.

FOCAL POINT WITH WORDS AND IMAGE

Always ensure that the words and the image work together to reinforce the focal point. In this rough design, the left-of-centre text placement is balanced by the extension of the wash to the right. This ensures that the focal point in the darkest wash area is maintained.

Focal point links foreground, middle ground, and sky

Passive middle ground balances relative activity of foreground and sky

THERE'S A WHISPER DOWN THE FIELD, WHERE THE YEAR HAS SHOT HER YIELD, AND THE RICKS STAND GREY TO THE SUN, SINGING, "OVER THEN, COME OVER, FOR THE BEE HAS QUIT THE CLOVER, & YOUR ENGLISH SUMMER'S DONE."

Placement of text helps to emphasize foreground detail

Diagonal sweep of furrows draws eye towards focal point

A FINISHED COMPOSITION

In this piece of illustrated calligraphy, the composition was carefully planned around the focal point formed by the flock of birds. The furrows of the ploughed field draw the eye across the text in the foreground to this point. This diagonal movement also provides a link across the horizontal divisions of the sky and landscape.

The use of colour enhances the unity of the composition, with the purple-brown of the text echoing both the browns of the fields and the indigo of the sky.

131

5

Projects

M ost calligraphers will, sooner or later, be required to design an invitation, and, even if you are new to calligraphy, you will be able to produce an attractive example with a well-written formal script. With greater experience, a wide variety of more challenging and exciting design possibilities will emerge, such

Invitation

PROJECTS

Choosing a script •

Determining the size •

Selecting the format •

as asymmetrical layouts, and contrasts of formal and free writing. Formal invitations can be greatly enhanced by calligraphy, used alone or combined with type. Handwritten letters and simple letter decoration — usually created by flourishing (see pp. 108–113) — can add the individual touch that type alone lacks.

Formal scripts, such as italic, are suitable for occasions such as weddings, christenings or banquets, but there are no hard-and-fast rules. The invitation could be written entirely in capitals, or in areas of upper- and lowercase letters to suit the text and overall design. You might combine compatible scripts, use a suitably embellished capital, change to a larger nib for names or write them in a different script.

Designing an invitation for printing means preparing artwork in the form of a paste-up, with calligraphy written in black and with colour instructions for the printer. If you are reproducing the invitations by photocopying, they can be copied in black and white or colour on to white or coloured paper thick enough to cut or fold into cards. Your invitation will usually need to comply to a regular size and shape used by the printer, and, if you work larger, you will have to prepare your artwork to scale (see "Sizing up", p. 48).

The wedding invitation shown here had to give prominence to the names of the bride and the groom, while conveying varying levels of information about the wedding and reception clearly and attractively.

Suzanne and Frank Brown
request the pleasure of your company
at the marriage of their daughter
Miranda
to
Mr. Steven Johnson
on Saturday, the twelfth of June
nineteen hundred and ninety-three
at eleven in the morning
St. Margaret's Church
Bennington, Vermont
and afterwards at the reception
The Laurels 517 Chestnut Drive

THE PRINTED INVITATION
The invitation is printed on a white card with a silver deckled edge. The result is elegant and restrained.

THUMBNAILS

The first step in the planning process is to sketch out layout alternatives from the text supplied. At this stage, the format of the invitation and the distribution of the words within that format are the main concerns. Four options, all with centred text, are tried. The wide vertical format is selected for development.

Square format

Narrow vertical format

Wide vertical format

Horizontal format

EXPERIMENTING WITH LETTERFORMS

Italic minuscules and capitals — being both formal and decorative — were the obvious choice for this kind of occasion. The precise details of width and spacing, however, need to be worked out. An all-capitals version and three versions of the minuscules from wide to narrow are tried.

Suzanne and Frank Brown
Compressed italic minuscules with capitals

Suzanne and Frank Brown
Compressed and sharpened italic minuscules with capitals

Suzanne and Frank Brown
Standard italic minuscules

SUZANNE & FRANK BROWN
Italic capitals with slight flourishes

CHOOSING THE PAPER

The choice of paper or card for calligraphic work that is to be printed is subject to considerations that are different from those taken into account when selecting a surface to write on (see pp. 36–37). For printed work you are primarily concerned with colour, weight, and texture. Obtain samples from the printer and judge them in relation to the colour of ink you are using and the overall effect you are aiming to achieve.

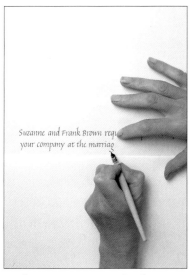

1 *The text is written in the chosen version of italic with a Mitchell No. 4 nib to 5 nib widths x height. Writing of this size is designed to be reduced in printing to the dimensions of the finished invitation.*

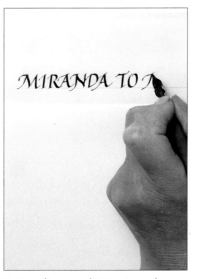

2 *A preliminary decision is made to render the names of the bridal couple in swash capitals, using a Mitchell No. 3 nib.*

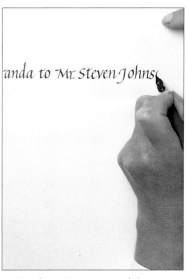

3 *An alternative version of the names in italic minuscules, also in the larger nib size, is tried for comparison.*

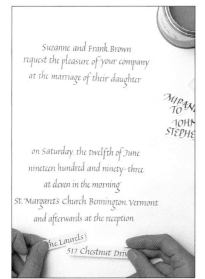

4 *The text is cut into lines and a paste-up is started with spacing assessed by eye. When the arrangement is judged to be right, accurately measured lines can be ruled to guide the final paste-up.*

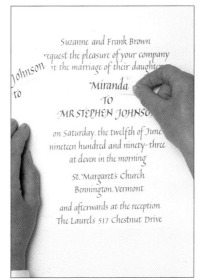

5 *Once the capitalized version of the couple's names is pasted up, it is compared with the minuscule version. The decision is made to substitute the minuscule script.*

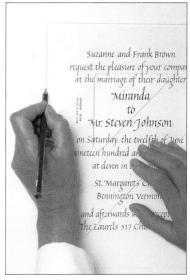

6 *With all the text satisfactorily pasted in position, margins are ruled in blue pencil to show the printer the final proportions required. The margins must be in proportion to the size of the final printed invitation.*

Gallery

Calligraphy in invitation design can be used on its own or in harmony with type. Flourishes are a natural choice for calligraphic enhancement of invitations, but other decorative elements may also be used to great effect. Sensitivity of design can extend to the choice of paper, the way in which the invitation is folded and the addressing of the envelope. Creating invitations is an excellent way of putting calligraphy to practical use.

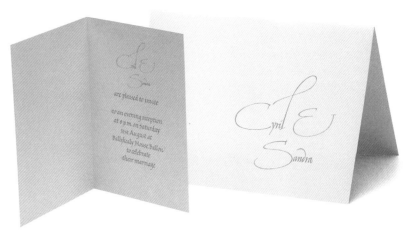

MATCHING INVITATIONS — Angela Hickey

This pair of wedding invitations — one to the wedding, the other to the reception — shows the elegant use of flourished italics.

Mr. & Mrs Michael Knight
request the pleasure of the company of

at the marriage of their daughter
Helen Louise
to
Andrew Ronald Raymant

at the parish church of St Michael
Chenies, Buckinghamshire
on Saturday 27th July
at 2·00 p.m
and afterwards at a reception
at Chenies Manor House until 7·30 p.m

RSVP. 7 Hamble Close, Ruislip, Middlesex HA4 7EP

DECORATED INVITATION — Timothy Noad

In this original design for a wedding invitation, simple decorative motifs provide added interest. The text is written in formal italic, with emphasis provided by changes of scale.

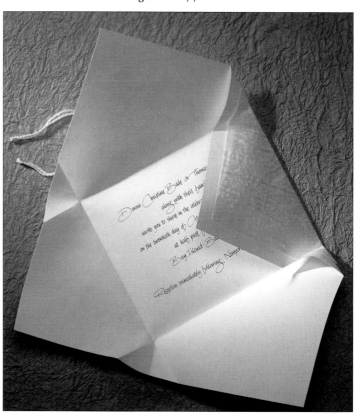

WEDDING INVITATION — Bonnie Leah

This delicate design is printed on fine-quality white paper, with an original touch added by the use of Japanese lace-paper backing. Folded dimensions: 13.5 cm × 10 cm (5¼" × 4").

Designing a letterhead is a rewarding and straightforward project for calligraphy beginners to tackle. This exercise can also provide interesting design challenges for slightly more advanced calligraphers who have a greater number of scripts and decorative techniques at their disposal.

Letterhead

PROJECTS

Creating an identity •

Planning a logo •

Producing artwork for printing •

Calligraphy gives enormous scope as to the script, layout and design choices available, making it invaluable for creating a unique look for a letterhead. You will need to consider which type of lettering will be most appropriate to the person or business whose letterhead you are designing. Do you want the letterhead to look quiet and formal, or eye-catching and lively? If the former, either foundational hand or formal italic would be a good choice. If the latter, a vigorously written cursive italic might be suitable.

A further element that you may wish to incorporate is a motif or logo. This could be a simple graphic device or a sophisticated illustration, depending on your skill and the requirements of your client.

The placement of each element in the design in relation to the whole needs to be carefully worked out. Do you want a close vertical texture for impact, or wide line spacing for elegance? Is the alignment to be to the right, left, centred or asymmetrical? And how is the letterhead to be placed on the page?

Beyond the design considerations, you also have to plan how the artwork is to be submitted to the printer. A preliminary discussion with the printer to establish the requirements can avoid expensive mistakes.

The letterhead project shown on the following pages is for a ceramics studio. It needed to convey the handcrafted character of a professional business.

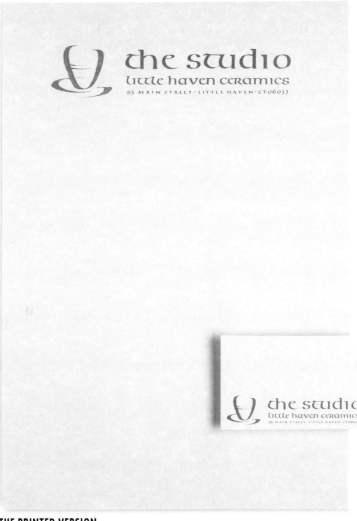

THE PRINTED VERSION
Calligraphic lettering provides an original company identity that can be used on a letterhead and a business card.

SELECTING A SCRIPT

The first task is to choose a script in
keeping with the image that the person
or business wants to project. Uncials
or half uncials seem good first choices
with their craft-based associations.
Various scripts are tried.

the studio

LIttLe haven

Serifed uncials at 4½ nib widths

the studio

little háven

Half uncials at 4 nib widths

the studio

little haven

Uncials at 3½ nib widths

ALTERNATIVE LAYOUTS

Having decided on a script, the next
stage is to work out a layout. The
main issues to be determined at this
stage are the size of the lettering and
its alignment. Rough pencil sketches
are adequate for this purpose. It is
decided that the name of the business
should be rendered in the largest size.
The relative size of the rest of the text
needs to be worked out. Experiments
with a logo are also tried at this stage.

Centred layout, two text sizes

Ragged left-aligned layout, three text sizes

Left-aligned layout with logo, three text sizes

Right-aligned layout, three text sizes

THE FINAL DESIGN

Elements of the second and third
layouts (above) have been incorporated
into the final design. The text
arrangement of the second layout
(with slight adjustments to text size)
is combined with the logo suggestion
of the third. The letterhead is to be
centred on the paper.

Centred layout

All lettering in half uncials

Three sizes of text

Pen-drawn logo

139

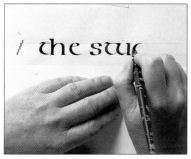

1 *The writing of the large-size lettering is started between lines ruled to 4 nib widths. A Mitchell No. 0 nib is used, producing lettering that is larger than it will appear in the final printed form. Reduction sharpens the letterforms.*

2 *As the letterhead is to be printed from a paste-up, small imperfections can be painted out in opaque white. This is a bleed-proof paint that covers any underlying ink effectively.*

3 *The artwork for the logo is drawn using a Mitchell No. 0 nib. A textured watercolour paper is used, which gives a rough appearance to the work.*

4 *Final adjustments to the layout are made before pasting up the lettering and artwork. Guidelines for the paste-up are ruled.*

5 *Photocopies of each element — reduced in size where necessary — are pasted carefully in position to show the final effect.*

6 *The intended size of each element is measured from the paste-up and calculated as a percentage of the original so that instructions can be given for a PMT (photomechanical-transfer) reduction.*

7 *The exact positions of the artwork and lettering are also measured from the paste-up and noted.*

8 *The margins and precise guidelines for the positioning of the letterhead on the paper are marked for a final "camera-ready" paste-up for the printer. Non-reproducible blue pencil, which will not show in the printing, is used.*

9 *The final paste-up of the artwork is completed for printing. Instructions on colour and paper type are given to the printer separately.*

Gallery

Letterheads provide a design challenge. Whether you are commissioned to design a formal and understated piece, or something eye-catching, the creation of an appropriate image is an excellent opportunity to practise your design skills. The letterheads by experienced calligraphers on this page illustrate some of the interesting possibilities available.

BONNIE LEAH LETTERING AND DESIGN

1801 DOVE STREET SUITE 104

NEWPORT BEACH CA 92660

714·752·7820

RIBBON-DECORATED LETTERHEAD
Bonnie Leah

This delicate stationery design (above) shows the sensitive combination of decorated calligraphic letterforms and type. The diamond shape and ribbon decoration provide an original touch. Dimensions: 28 cm × 22 cm (11″ × 8½″).

GEORGIA DEAVER

Elizabeth Rounce calligraphic lettering & design · 39 selwyn avenue richmond surrey TW9 2HB · 081 940 6442

Christopher Haanes · F.S.S.I.

Kalligrafisk Design & Skriftkunst

Hesselberggt. 3 · N-0555

OSLO · NORWAY

Tel./fax.: 02-35 41 23

Selvst. næring nr. 309 909 19

Postgiro 0531 63 28611

VERTICAL LETTERHEAD
Christopher Haanes

The combination of lively flourished italic with red type makes for a sophisticated image. Further interest is created by the vertical placement of the calligraphy.

PRINTED LETTERHEADS
Georgia Deaver (above left) and
Elizabeth Rounce (below left)

These examples show how careful attention to contrasts of weight and scale can provide great impact.

A broadsheet is a single sheet of paper containing text. This can be a single poem or section of a poem, several poems, or prose, and can be linked by a theme. A broadsheet design should not be too complicated, or it may detract from the meaning of the text. A simple approach is usually the key to success.

Poetry broadsheet

PROJECTS

Arranging text elements •

Harmonizing script and illustration •

Displaying the finished piece •

The broadsheet is a useful project for the inexperienced calligrapher, and one to which you can return as you progress, because it offers plenty of opportunity for practising newly acquired skills and using them creatively. Working on texts and themes will help you to release and develop your imagination, and find ways of interpreting your personal reactions to the passages you choose to write. This can be a stimulating experience and a source of fun. A finished broadsheet can be framed and displayed. The choice of quotations is crucial, and a personal interest in the theme will give the work excitement and a sense of discovery. If you enjoy the time that you spend working on the project, this will communicate itself to the viewer.

In the broadsheet shown here, texts were "hung" around a central piece of writing. The calligrapher was fascinated by the sense of wildness and the closeness with nature reflected in some early Irish poems. The core text was powerful and deeply imaginative, and the additional quotations enhanced this feeling while also creating atmosphere. The theme linked the contrasts of beauty and harshness in a landscape integrally bound up with the lives of its inhabitant birds and animals. The scripts were chosen to create an inter-play between the central and the surrounding texts, while harmonious colours, repeated shapes and images and gentle contrasts served to unify the design as a whole.

THE FINISHED WORK
The completed panel shows a delicate harmony of text and illustration. To display the work, a natural limed-wood frame is selected, whose muted colour does not overwhelm the subtle lettering colours.

THE EVOLVING IDEA

The initial design ideas for both the text and the illustration in this project are developed simultaneously. The calligrapher sketches broad areas to represent the component elements, so that the final design will form a unified whole.

The design is a triptych, with the main text placed centrally and the two subsidiary texts on either side. At this stage, the calligrapher's notes indicate that she intends the focus of the piece to be reinforced by rendering the main text in a darker tone than that of the subsidiary texts — a decision that is later partially reversed.

The thumbnail sketches with their accompanying notes show the development of the illustration ideas.

THE FINAL ROUGH

The calligrapher refines her ideas in a rough layout, in which she determines the positions of the three component poems and the illustration areas. The text is rendered in italic script and in colours approximating those to be used in the finished piece, in order to make the rough as accurate as possible.

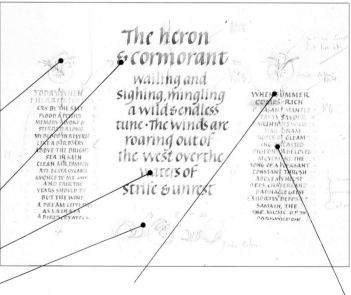

Bird illustration

Main heading: italic minuscules, Mitchell No. 1½ nib

Main poem: italic minuscules, Mitchell No. 2½ nib, centred

Wave illustration

Subsidiary headings: italic capitals, Mitchell No. 4 nib, paler than main heading

Subsidiary poems: italic capitals, Mitchell No. 6 nib, centred, same colour as main text

143

1 *The initial writing of the text uses the selected colours in order to judge their effect. Different colours are tried on scraps of paper first.*

2 *Photocopies of the text are cut out and pasted in position. The central panel is placed first. Care is taken to ensure that the panels are evenly balanced with equal numbers of lines. Several attempts are needed.*

3 *With all the elements placed in position, measurements of the line spacing are taken from the paste-up to be transferred to the final version.*

4 *Further work is needed on the illustrations. The calligrapher experiments with different colour treatments before making a final decision. Here, a muted yellow wash is painted over a pencil drawing.*

5 *The final writing is started. The central panel is completed first, because its position determines the placement of the other elements.*

6 *Using the paste-up as a guide, ruled lines to mark the position of the side panels are drawn in relation to the central panel.*

7 *The side panels are written along the ruled guidelines.*

8 *The illustrations are the last element to be added. They are carefully drawn in pencil before the coloured washes are put in.*

9 *A final decision on margins is made once the work is completed. L-shaped cards are used to judge the margins, and these are pencilled in. The broadsheet is later trimmed, and a mount is added for display.*

Most of the panels of poetry shown in this gallery are examples of personal responses to the text, expressed in calligraphic terms. For calligraphers at all levels, poetry and literature in general can serve as a major stimulus for experimental creative work. Working from soundly understood letterforms, you can use poetry to explore variations in weight, slant and layout. Colour, too, can be brought into play as a means of expressing the mood of the poem, from bright and energetic to quietly harmonious — the choice belongs to the calligrapher.

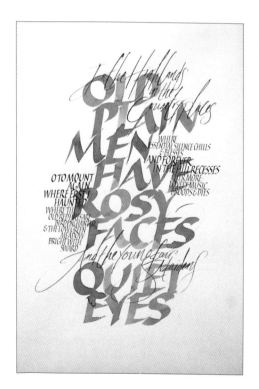

IN THE HIGHLANDS — Louise Donaldson

This calligraphic panel, based on a poem by Robert Louis Stevenson, uses different styles and sizes of lettering. Dimensions: 64 cm × 40.5 cm (26″ × 16½″).

THE FISH — Janet Mehigan

Written in gouache in a light-weight italic script, this rendering of a poem by Rupert Brooke is an example of a simple layout. Dimensions: 98 cm × 47 cm (40″ × 19″).

145

CROSSROADS – Nancy R. Leavitt

This imaginative interpretation of a text by Karl Young (above) uses a close-knit vertical texture of different-sized versals. Colour changes set off the lettering from the background, which links the various elements of the design. Dimensions: 36 cm × 22 cm (14″ × 8¾″).

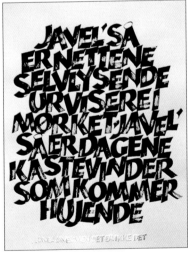

JAVEL – Julia Vance

The use of heavy-weight dancing capitals with close interline spacing (above) creates a lively graphic effect. The small gilded capitals provide an interesting contrast within the design. Dimensions: 51 cm × 61 cm (20″ × 24″).

ONE IN ALL, ALL IN ONE – Paivi Vesanto

The compressed slanting letters of this italic-based script (above) give a strong diagonal emphasis to the design. The exaggerated open letters left uncoloured on a Conté-crayon background produce an interesting change of texture. Dimensions: 23 cm × 69 cm (9″ × 27″).

TOR HOUSE

ROBINSON JEFFERS

IF YOU SHOULD LOOK FOR THIS PLACE
AFTER A HANDFUL OF LIFETIMES;
PERHAPS OF MY PLANTED FOREST A FEW
MAY STAND YET,
DARK-LEAVED AUSTRALIANS
OR THE COAST CYPRESS, HAGGARD
WITH STORM-DRIFT;
BUT FIRE AND THE AXE ARE DEVILS.

YOU WILL KNOW IT
BY THE WILD SEA-FRAGRANCE OF WIND
THOUGH THE OCEAN MAY HAVE CLIMBED
OR RETIRED A LITTLE;
YOU WILL KNOW IT
BY THE VALLEY INLAND THAT
OUR SUN AND OUR MOON
WERE BORN FROM
BEFORE THE POLES CHANGED;
AND ORION IN DECEMBER
EVENINGS WAS STRUNG IN THE THROAT OF
THE VALLEY LIKE A LAMPLIGHTED BRIDGE.

LOOK FOR FOUNDATIONS OF
SEA-WORN GRANITE
MY FINGERS HAD THE ART
TO MAKE STONE LOVE STONE
YOU WILL FIND SOME REMNANT.

COME IN THE MORNING
YOU WILL SEE WHITE GULLS
WEAVING A DANCE OVER BLUE WATER
THE WANE OF THE MOON
THEIR DANCE-COMPANION,
A GHOST WALKING
BY DAYLIGHT,
BUT WILDER AND WHITER THAN
ANY BIRD IN THE WORLD.

BUT IF YOU SHOULD LOOK IN YOUR IDLENESS AFTER
TEN·THOUSAND·YEARS;
IT IS THE GRANITE KNOLL
ON THE GRANITE AND LAVA TONGUE
IN THE MIDST OF THE BAY,
BY THE MOUTH OF THE CARMEL
RIVER VALLEY
THESE FOUR WILL REMAIN
IN THE CHANGE OF NAMES.

MY GHOST YOU NEEDN'T LOOK FOR;
IT IS PROBABLY
HERE, BUT A DARK ONE,
DEEP IN THE GRANITE,
NOT DANCING ON WIND
WITH THE MAD WINGS AND THE DAY MOON

RIDDLE

I STRETCH BEYOND THE BOUNDS OF THE WORLD,
I'M SMALLER THAN A WORM,
OUTSTRIP THE SUN,
I SHINE MORE BRIGHTLY THAN THE MOON,
THE SWELLING SEAS
THE FAIR FACE OF THE EARTH
AND ALL THE GREEN FIELDS
ARE WITHIN MY CLASP, I COVER THE DEPTHS
AND PLUNGE BENEATH HELL,
I ASCEND ABOVE HEAVEN
HIGHLAND OF RENOWN, I REACH BEYOND
THE BOUNDARIES
OF THE LAND OF BLESSED ANGELS,
I FILL FAR AND WIDE THE CORNERS OF THE EARTH
AND THE OCEAN STREAMS

SAY WHAT MY NAME IS

FROM THE EXETER BOOK OF RIDDLES TRANSLATED BY KEVIN CROSSLEY-HOLLAND

TOR HOUSE – Sheila Waters

A wide range of capitals is used in this interpretation of a poem by Robinson Jeffers (above). Changes in weight, size and compression provide subtle variations in emphasis. The delicate colour of the vellum gently unites the text areas. Dimensions: 58 cm × 39 cm (23″ × 15½″).

CREATION – Gillian Hazeldine

This text from the Exeter Book of Riddles *(left) is rendered in heavy-weight capitals with a scattering of light-weight Roman capitals, creating an interesting overall texture. The asymmetrical layout adds to the sense of movement. Dimensions: 45 cm × 30 cm (17¾″ × 12″).*

Calligraphy can be a striking alternative or complement to print in poster design. A calligraphic poster is a challenge, whatever your level of skill, giving you the chance to put your writing and design abilities to practical use. Whatever its specific aim, the successful poster should catch the eye of the intended

PROJECTS **Poster**

**Producing a design that
works well in two colours ●**

**Organizing the information into an
eye-catching, easy-to-read form ●**

audience and present the essential information clearly, so that it can be easily read at a quick glance. A poster can be reproduced at low cost and look attractive, even if it has to be in a single colour. Designing for one colour can stimulate imaginative use both of contrasts created by the lettering itself and of the space in and around the text. Colour can be introduced, if required, by printing on coloured paper or adding a splash of colour by hand to each poster.

Some posters suffer from "over-load", with too much happening and no focus; others are simply dull. You can use lettering alone to create an eye-catching focus, or choose suitable imagery to fulfil this role. It is important to create an atmosphere in the poster that is suited to the subject by wise choice of styles and sizes of lettering, and by considered use of space and illustration (if needed). Whatever the subject — whether you are creating a notice for a classical concert or an announcement for a contemporary-dance performance — all the design elements in the poster must be carefully selected and balanced.

In posters, as in all design, there are no absolute rules, but experience provides helpful hints. The poster shown here is a low-budget design for a jazz concert, to be printed in black on a photocopier. The poster needs to suggest a dynamic atmosphere while conveying a clear and eye-catching message.

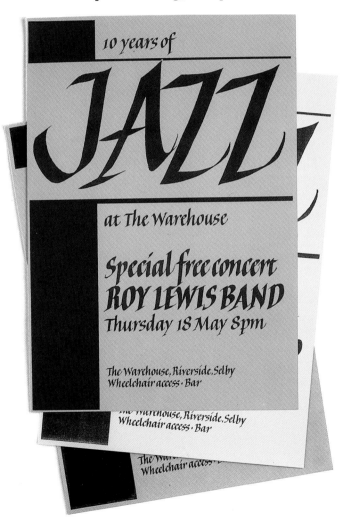

PRINTED POSTERS
*The finished calligraphic artwork is seen here
printed on to different coloured papers. The
green paper is selected for the final print run.*

ASSESSING THE TEXT

In most cases the client supplies the text for the poster, as in this case, in the form of typed copy. The first task is to organize the information into "bite-size" pieces and sort them according to their relative importance. Here, the calligrapher also suggests ways of making the wording punchier.

TENTH ANNIVERSARY OF JAZZ AT THE WAREHOUSE

SPECIAL FREE CONCERT ~~WITH~~ ROY LEWIS BAND

~~ON~~ THURSDAY 18th MAY ~~AT~~ 8pm ~~AT~~ THE WAREHOUSE

RIVERSIDE SELBY ~~NOTE:~~ FACILITIES FOR

WHEELCHAIR ACCESS

WHEELCHAIRS ~~AND~~ BAR

THUMBNAIL SKETCHES

Various layout ideas are tried, incorporating different sizes and styles of lettering. The word "JAZZ" is picked out to provide the main focus of the overall design.

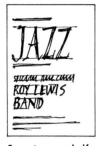

Horizontal orientation, upturned lettering at left margin

Focus in lower half of design with diagonal subsidiary elements

Focus in upper half, aligned left

Focus in upper half, aligned left to solid band in margin

Focus in upper half, main lettering breaking into band in left margin

Focus in upper half, solid bands at top and bottom, aligned left

THE FINAL DESIGN

The final thumbnail 5 (above) provides the best combination of elements, with the broken black band providing contrast and emphasis, leading the eye down the poster to the subsidiary information. In this final rough (right), the addition of horizontal lines above and below the word "JAZZ" strengthens the focus. At this point, decisions on letterform, weight and size are firmed up. All the lettering is in compressed italic, which conveys an appropriate sense of controlled energy. Variations in size and weight provide different levels of emphasis.

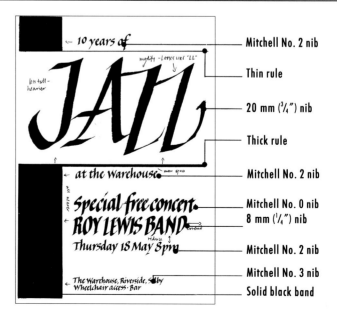

- Mitchell No. 2 nib
- Thin rule
- 20 mm (³/₄") nib
- Thick rule
- Mitchell No. 2 nib
- Mitchell No. 0 nib
- 8 mm (¹/₄") nib
- Mitchell No. 2 nib
- Mitchell No. 3 nib
- Solid black band

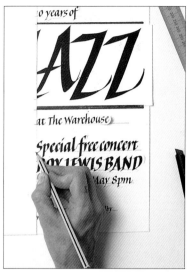

1 *The text is written out in preparation for a preliminary paste-up. At this point it is still possible to fine-tune the size and weight of the lettering. Here, the main word is written using a 13 mm (¹/₂″) Automatic pen. On consideration, this does not seem strong enough.*

2 *A paste-up is completed using photocopies of the lettering. "JAZZ" has been re-written using a 20 mm (³/₄″) nib. At this stage, fine adjustments of text position are made.*

3 *Measurements of line spacing are taken from the paste-up and transferred to the final (camera-ready) paste-up.*

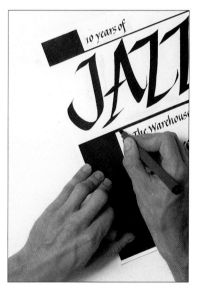

4 *The text is placed in its final position on the final paste-up.*

5 *The black bands and rules are carefully drawn in with indelible felt-tip pens. Any marks and imperfections — including the edges of the pasted-up text — are obliterated using correction fluid (or opaque white paint).*

6 *A fine marker pen is used to fill any unevenness in the rules and to ensure the black areas are "solid". The poster is now ready for reproduction. At this stage, the choice to print on white or coloured paper is made.*

150

Gallery

Calligraphic lettering used in poster design can create a visual impact quite different from that which can be achieved with type alone. Key words can be rendered in a style that is specifically designed to be in harmony with the overall message. Extra-broad plain-stroke or multiline pens can be used to great effect in a design where one eye-catching word or image is required. This is also an area where you can adapt the letterforms or create new forms of your own, if this seems appropriate. With posters, the freshness of the image is the key consideration.

CREATIVE STUDIES — Jenny Kavarana

This exhibition poster (above) uses bold white lettering based on Rudolf Koch's "Neuland" alphabet, with a dark background. Close interline spacing and subtle use of colour between the letters makes for a striking design. Dimensions: 61 cm × 43 cm (24″ × 17″).

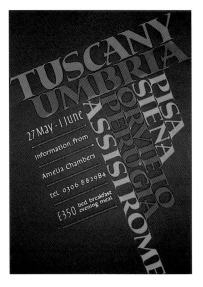

EXHIBITION POSTER — Louise Donaldson

This attractive piece of work (above) uses ruling-pen lettering in masking fluid under a gradated wash, alongside edged-pen calligraphy. Dimensions: 66 cm × 40.5 cm (26″ × 16½).

TUSCANY — Jenny Kavarana

The diagonal lines of text, bold capitals, strong colours and a dark background (left) all contribute to the strong image. The small white lettering makes a pleasing contrast and is united with the rest of the design by the ruled red lines. Dimensions: 61 cm × 43 cm (24″ × 17″).

This type of simple folded book, which is also a display panel, is a popular application for calligraphy. It combines the opportunity of using a relatively long text at a convenient size with the challenge of having to design pages that work well when fully opened, as well as individually. The need for the design to flow

PROJECTS

Concertina book

Enhancing text through layout •

Using stencil illustration •

Making a closing cover •

horizontally through the book provides some interesting possibilities for both the calligraphy and the illustration. Colour can often provide a unifying element through the book.

Any page proportion is possible with a concertina book, making it an interesting design vehicle for unifying the mood of the text and the mode of presentation. Margin proportions can be varied to enhance interpretation — a text about open spaces might have a very wide top margin, for example.

The concertina book shown here makes use of an anonymous medieval poem about the seasons. The simplicity of the words seems to lend itself well to this intimate treatment, and the continuous nature of a concertina book works well with the idea of the seasonal cycle.

THE FINISHED BOOK
This horizontal-format book folds neatly into its cover. As the cover is fixed only at the front, the book can be opened and extended to show all its pages at a single view.

INITIAL LAYOUTS

The decision has already been made to use a horizontal format with illustrations based on the medieval symbols for the seasons. However, the size of the lettering, the relationship of the headings to the text and the position and treatment of the motif need to be worked out in greater detail.

Various rough layouts are tried. The position of the motif at the left of the page remains constant, as does the rendering of the text in italic capitals. The major questions to be resolved are the size, weight and spacing of the text. The rough layouts at right show the evolution of the idea, although none of these solutions is eventually selected for development. The idea of widely spaced lettering for the heading proves too weak, and a more conventional letter spacing is adopted.

S P R I N G
FOR LAVENDER, BUSHY SWEET AND TALL
TEND UPON THE FEAST OF SAINT PAUL

S P R I N G
FOR LAVENDER BUSHY SWEET AND TALL
TEND UPON THE FEAST OF SAINT PAUL

S P R I N G
FOR LAVENDER BUSHY, SWEET AND TALL
TEND UPON THE FEAST OF SAINT PAUL

S P R I N G
FOR LAVENDER BUSHY SWEET AND TALL
TEND UPON THE FEAST OF SAINT PAUL

1 *The text is written and pasted up with the pen-drawn symbol. The verse is written with a Mitchell No. 4 nib and the heading with a No. 2½. At this stage, the final decision on the letter spacing of the heading is made.*

2 *The final paste-up shows the arrangement of the symbol, heading and verse on the page. A paste-up is needed for each page.*

3 *Final choices of paper and colour are made. The project requires a paper that is suitable for both ink and watercolour. A pale-cream textured paper is chosen after testing the selected colours on it.*

4 *The motifs are to be stencilled. The first stage is to trace each pen-drawn motif in pencil.*

5 *A piece of low-tack masking film is adhered over the tracing.*

6 *A craft knife is used to cut out the traced symbol, following the drawn outlines accurately.*

7 *The masking film is carefully peeled away from the tracing paper, and placed so that the symbol is in its final position on the paper. The surrounding paper is carefully masked. The chosen colours are mixed and spattered over the stencil using a stencil brush.*

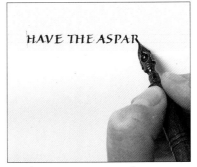

8 *The text is written on the pages in black ink, in the positions specified by the final paste-up.*

9 *The cover is cut to allow 3 mm (⅛″) extra at the top and bottom, plus 13 mm (½″) at the front and a 25 mm (1″) flap with 50 mm (2″) tab at the back (see p. 152). The folds of the cover are scored (see also p. 159). The front flap is glued to the first page only.*

Gallery

The different concertina books illustrated on this page indicate the wide scope open to you in designing a concertina book. As the examples show, this type of book is an attractive and manageable project for a calligraphy beginner.

LOVE — Mary Noble

This unusual book (above) consists of two concertina sheets with slits that are slotted together vertically. Dimensions (opened): 25.5 cm × 64 cm (10″ × 25″).

ANGLO-SAXON RIDDLE — Anne Irwin

The well-planned simplicity of this concertina book (left) is the key to its success. Rubber-stamp motifs are used alongside text written in a basic Roman bookhand. Dimensions (opened): 7.5 cm × 275 cm (3″ × 108″).

ZODIAC — Patricia Lovett

This attractive concertina book (above), based on the signs of the zodiac, incorporates subtle illustrations over painted background squares. Dimensions: 12.5 cm × 20.5 cm (5″ × 8″).

B ooks in the form of the "codex", or book form as we know it today were handwritten from Roman times until the Renaissance, and, even after the invention of printing, rich patrons still commissioned manuscript volumes. The manuscript book continues to offer useful design experience to calligraphers

Manuscript book

PROJECTS **5**

at all levels, posing questions about the relationship between text area and margins, page size and shape, length of writing line, size, weight and styles of writing, and the choice of writing and binding materials. Different paper surfaces can also be explored. Although hot-pressed paper is the easiest to write on and most suitable for a formal manuscript book, a more textural surface can greatly enhance the atmosphere of a text whose words lend themselves to this approach.

Even the beginner can make an attractive manuscript book, because the book lends itself just as well to the straightforward treatment of a short text as to longer and more elaborate writing and designs. Books can be one or many sections, and illustration can range from a simple decorative element, such as a symbol, to ornate illumination. A single section is best for a first book. Traditionally, this consists of 16 pages — including a title page and several blank pages at the beginning and end of the book, so that there are about five to seven pages of writing — but there can be fewer if you prefer. You can include a discreet colophon at the back of the book, giving your name and the date of writing. You can then sew on a simple cover with or without decoration.

Any page proportion is possible, and your eye is the final arbiter. However, handwritten books usually look most effective with generous margins

The text selected for this manuscript book is a short and light-hearted essay by an Irish writer, John B. Keane, taken from his collection *Strong Tea.*

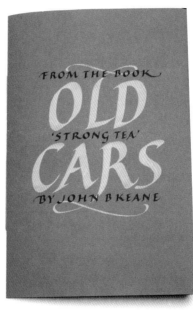

THE FINISHED BOOK
The cover, with its simple but decorative lettering (left), harmonizes with the straightforward calligraphy of the inside pages (below).

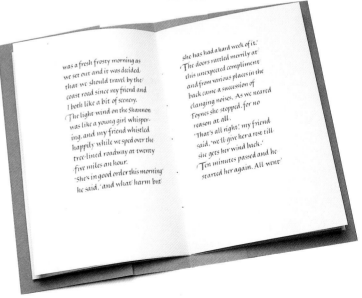

DETERMINING FORMAT AND PAGE SIZE

After reading the text and getting a feeling for its overall character, jot down some preliminary layout ideas. At this stage, you should consider format, page size and first thoughts on the script to be used. Note that at this stage it is important to work with double-page spreads.

The thumbnail sketches shown at right indicate some of the options tried for this project. After reviewing these possibilities, the calligrapher decides to pursue a relatively wide vertical format.

Large-capital start,
left-aligned text

Narrow vertical
format

Centred-capital start

Drop-capital start

Wider vertical format

Horizontal format

Spaced-capital start

WORKING OUT THE LETTERFORMS

Having decided on the format, it is possible to work out the treatment of the text in more detail. Although the text is humorous, it is decided not to over-emphasize this by using a zany script. A plain italic has the right feeling of simplicity. However, to give texture to the page and to provide variation in pace, larger coloured capitals are chosen for the paragraph openings. Experiments for these are shown at right.

WORKING OUT MARGINS

The margins of a manuscript book are calculated in a different way from those of a calligraphic panel. As a beginner, you should follow the standard formula for producing margins, in which the outer margin is twice the inner one and the bottom margin is twice the top margin.

1 *Draw an accurate double-page layout to your chosen page size.*

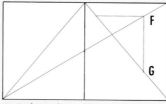

2 *Draw diagonals between points A, B, C and D, as shown.*

3 *Mark the top margin with a horizontal between E and F.*

4 *Rule in the right margin with a right-angle from F to G.*

5 *Rule in the remaining margins. The left-hand page mirrors the right.*

1 *Using a Mitchell No. 4 nib and black watercolour, the calligrapher writes out the text for a rough paste-up.*

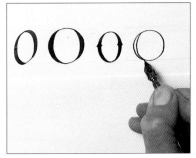

2 *Various styles — italic and versal — of introductory capitals are tried at different sizes.*

3 *Margins are ruled on a sheet of paper for the paste-up.*

4 *Lines that will act as guides for the paste-up are ruled, based on preliminary decisions made when selecting the letterform.*

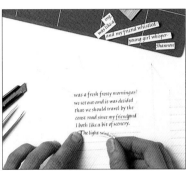

5 *The written-out text is cut out and pasted in position on the writing lines. Tweezers are useful for picking up and positioning small pieces of text.*

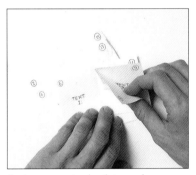

6 *A manuscript book is made up of sheets folded in half — each comprising four pages of the book. These are called folios. It is a good idea to prepare a miniature book that allows you to check and number the pages.*

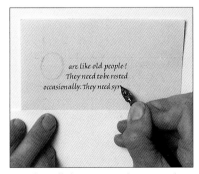

7 *After all decisions on layout and pagination have been made, the next stage is the final writing. With the versal capital pencilled in, the small black lettering is written first.*

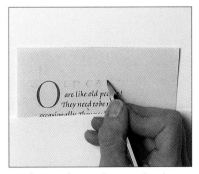

8 *The versal capital is completed next in blue gouache, and the introduction in small capitals is pencilled in.*

9 *The small capitals are written in pen in blue gouache.*

MAKING A COVER

A manuscript book needs a well-made cover to protect the inner pages. It should be made from heavy paper that will withstand handling. Once you have trimmed and folded the cover (see right), sew it to the text pages as shown below.

FOLDING THE COVER

The cover should be larger than the page dimensions; allow about 6 mm–13 mm ($\frac{1}{4}$"–$\frac{1}{2}$") extra at the top, bottom and outside edges. Give the cover generous flaps of about two-thirds the cover width. Once the cover is cut, score the outside folds of the spine and flaps using a sharp tool such as a craft knife. Take care not to cut through the paper.

SEWING THE COVER

Carefully position the folded folios inside the cover. Pierce the stitch holes from the inside fold of the centre folio through the outside spine fold of the cover, as shown in the diagram. Using heavy-weight thread and a strong needle, pass the needle through the middle hole in the inside fold in the centre folio, leaving a long loose end. Continue to sew following the sequence illustrated. Be careful not to divide the thread as you pass through a hole for the second time. To finish, tie the two loose ends together inside the book and trim.

Cover width Cover width $\frac{2}{3}$ cover width

Fold Fold

Page dimensions

Fold $\frac{2}{3}$ cover width

Outside

Inside

10 Once the writing is complete, the pages are trimmed (if necessary) and assembled in the correct order. The book is then placed on the chosen cover paper, and the dimensions of the cover are measured and marked.

11 The trimmed cover and book are sewn together with strong thread (see above).

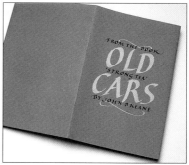

12 The finished book has a calligraphic cover that echoes the treatment of the inside pages.

Gallery

This selection of manuscript books illustrates a rich variety of approaches. It shows how a well-written classical format has great serenity and elegance, while a more experimental approach to the text has different strengths — most importantly, stimulating the inter-play of movement and stillness. This selection also demonstrates that beautifully written lettering has its own decorative quality, but that illustration sensitively blended with the text can enhance the overall design. Whether you choose a simple or complex design, making a manuscript book is a feasible project for calligraphers at every stage of learning. It is an intimate design vehicle for a thoughtful and personal approach.

THE PROTHALAMION – Hazel Dolby

This spread (above) combines grey gouache text and watercolour illustration. The generous margins enhance the delicacy of the whole. Dimensions: 34 cm × 25 cm (13½″ × 10″).

I take the word and go over it as though it were nothing more than human shape its arrangements awe me and I find my way through each variation in the spoken word — I utter and I am and without speaking I approach the limit of words and the silence.

the pure wine of language inexhaustable water

I drink to the word, raising a word or a shining cup, in it I drink the pure wine of language or inexhaustable water, maternal source of words, and cup and water and wine give rise to my song.

THE WORD – Kate Ridyard

In this book (above), the free italic-based script, written in red gouache with a ruling pen, contrasts strikingly with the black edged-pen italic. Dimensions (spread): 30.5 cm × 11.5 cm (12″ × 4½″).

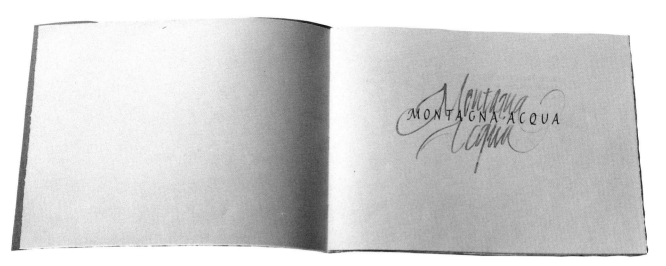

MONTAGNA-ACQUA — Monica Dengo

This title page from a book of the writings of François Cheng (above) shows an interesting design, created by contrasting formal-italic edged-pen capitals with a lively italic written with a ruling pen. Both ink and gouache are used. Dimensions: 20 cm × 26 cm (7⅛″ × 10⅝″)

SPEAK TO THE EARTH — Suzanne Moore

This centrefold (above) shows an unusual and sensitive presentation of a double-page spread. The close vertical texture of capitals balances and harmonizes with the illuminated symbol on the facing page, and the delicate flourishes on both pages further unite the spread. Dimensions (closed size): 42 cm × 27 cm (16½″ × 10½″).

FAIRY'S SONG — Joan Pilsbury

This elegant double-page spread (above) of a Shakespearean text written on vellum in formal italic shows the timeless quality of a well-written italic. The initial O is raised and burnished gold. The generous space around the text enhances the calm quality of the whole. Dimensions: 25 cm × 24.5 cm (10″ × 9¾″).

Although good calligraphy should be able to stand alone, there are situations in formal or creative work where decoration can enhance the written text. Decorative borders from Eastern and Western historical manuscripts are an infinitely varied source of reference for contemporary calligraphy. These borders may

PROJECTS

Decorative border

Designing simple illustration •

Balancing text and border •

Using colour effectively •

influence your own designs, but try to use them in new and creative ways. The wealth of designs in Western manuscripts includes simple coloured linear borders, which sometimes consist of different-coloured bands of varying widths. These may be plain, divided into decorated rectangles, or feature repeating patterns of geometric or inter-twined plant elements. Sometimes the border is an extension of a decorated initial letter. A myriad of plant designs, including complex floral designs, are found in Flemish, French and Italian manuscripts from the late medieval period onwards.

Possibilities for contemporary borders abound. Apart from plants and geometric shapes, patterns and symbols from different cultures or religions can be a source of ideas. Whatever the design, small illustrations can be introduced at intervals, perhaps enclosed in circles or other shapes.

As with any other form of decoration, the border must be appropriate to the subject and script, and form an integral part of the work as a whole. Plant borders may be contained by coloured or gilded lines of suitable width, or left with the plants themselves forming the outer edges of the design.

The floral border in this project is suitable for use in a manuscript book or, as shown here, could be displayed in a framed panel. The text, with its references to nature, seemed to suggest such a treatment.

In these vernal seasons of the year when the air is calm and pleasant it were an injury and sullenness against Nature not to go out and see her riches and partake in her rejoicing

THE FINISHED WORK
The delicate floral border, together with the elegant italic text, would be overwhelmed by a heavy frame and mount. A fine gold frame discreetly complements both the calligraphy and the decoration.

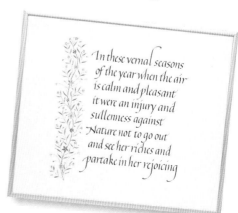

FIRST THOUGHTS

For this project, the first step is to decide on the page format and on the placement of the floral borders on the page.

Various options shown below are sketched as thumbnails. The final design is vertical with a single border along the left margin.

Border at left and below	Border below	Border on all sides	Border at top	Border at left

DESIGNING THE BORDER

The decision on the final design arises from trial illustrations. The choice is between designs of varying complexity, and whether to include repeating elements.

1 *Simple alternating flower-and-foliage motif with a strong central linear element.*

2 *Undulating central stem with non-repeating design.*

3 *Three-part design of non-repeating complex flower-and-stem pattern.*

4 *Complex flower-and-stem pattern with strong central emphasis. Repeating colour combinations.*

THE FINAL DESIGN

In the final layout, shown here as a rough paste-up, the border design shown in example 3 (above) is selected for development. The decision is made to use italics for the text, with simple flourishes at selected points to break up the outline. The colours used are clear and bright, but not so strong as to overwhelm the text.

In these vernal seasons
of the year when the air
is calm and pleasant
it were an injury and
sullenness against
Nature not to go out
and see her riches and
partake in her rejoicing

Italic text
with selective
flourishing using a
Mitchell No. 3 nib

Aligned left layout

Border along left
margin only

Dense floral design
with repeating colour
combinations

1 *The text is written for a final paste-up using a Mitchell No. 3 nib.*

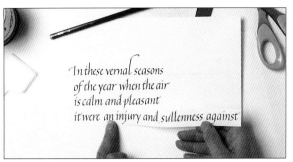

2 *The text is pasted up line by line. Each line is cut to length only when the line length is established.*

3 *The final writing out of the text follows the paste-up. A heavy, hot-pressed paper is used.*

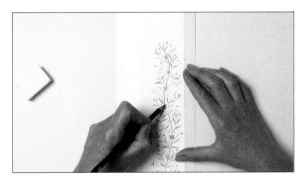

4 *A tracing is made of the chosen design for the floral border. Placing a pad of paper under the drawing will help you to obtain a good-quality line.*

5 *The traced design is transferred to its final position on the writing sheet by placing carbon paper between the tracing paper and the paper. Simply draw over the tracing, pressing firmly. Any unwanted marks can be removed from the paper with an eraser.*

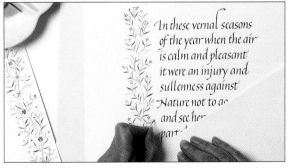

6 *The final illustration is coloured by applying watercolour with a fine brush.*

Gallery

Decorative borders have been a particularly attractive enhancement of calligraphic work for many centuries in both East and West. Whether realistic, stylized or invented, floral borders are particularly suited to flowing calligraphic forms. In Western manuscripts, such as Renaissance Books of Hours, the fine details of the painting and gilding are superb. In a simpler form, this kind of illustration is readily accessible to the calligraphy beginner. Whether you are creating a manuscript book or a panel of calligraphy, you will find it rewarding to combine border design with calligraphy.

CALLIGRAPHIC PANEL
Carina Westling

This panel of flowing cursive italic is enhanced by finely painted and gilded borders using an inter-laced design. The unusual decision to use two contrasting L-shapes creates an effective balance in conjunction with the circular focal decoration.

DRAPERS' COMPANY 500th-ANNIVERSARY CHARTER
Joan Pilsbury and Wendy Westover

This charter, written on vellum in italic with raised and burnished gold versal capitals, is a superb example of a formal document. The beautifully detailed watercolour and gouache borders use plant designs and heraldic elements with gold details. Dimensions: 168 cm × 137 cm (66″ × 54″).

REMEMBRANCE BOOK — Gaynor Goffe

This simple repeating border painted in gouache is one of a series in a book of remembrance. The border elements of this page are designed to reflect the life of the deceased. Dimensions: 25 cm × 18 cm (10″ × 7″).

Illuminated or decorated letters have been employed by calligraphers for nearly two thousand years to "light up" pages of text. In addition to this traditional application of decorative letterwork, designs based on a single letterform can also be used for greetings cards, letterheads and commemorative panels.

PROJECTS

Illuminated letter

Adapting a letterform •

Designing decoration •

Applying gold-transfer leaf •

Illuminated letters can encompass a vast array of different types of design, from the fantastic illustrated compositions of medieval manuscripts, through intricate scrollwork, to the colourful modern graphic treatments of this century. What all the best illuminated letters have in common is a harmony between the letterform and the decorative treatment.

You do not have to be an expert illustrator to try your hand at decorative lettering. You can start by copying ideas from early manuscripts (try to find a book of reproductions from a library or museum) and adapting them to your own requirements — using your own colour choices, for example. Later, try adding illustration ideas of your own. Simple plant forms are a great source of inspiration.

Using historical sources for guidance is an excellent way of learning about the tools and techniques of the craft, and about letterform design and illumination. However, the use of historical resources should not stop at analysing and copying, but rather this resource should be a springboard for developing you own contemporary ideas.

Versal letterforms were the traditional vehicle for medieval illumination; their built-up forms are ideal for the addition of colour or gilding. However, almost any script can be used in a modern context.

In the project shown on the following pages, a single letter was decorated using gouache and gilding. The intention was to produce a design for a greetings card.

FINISHED CARD
The completed letter (above) is mounted on green card from which a "window" has been cut. A greeting could be written on the plain paper fixed inside the card.

PLANNING THE ILLUSTRATION

The design is to be based around the letter Q using a form of versal script known as Lombardic. The letterform, with its spacious counter and graceful tail, provides ample opportunities for decoration within and around the letter. The scrolling form of the tail, in particular, provides a starting point for a design based on curling tendrils of vine leaves. A number of annotated sketches explore the possibilities for this type of design. A major decision to be made is how far to extend the decoration beyond the boundaries of the letterform.

THE FINAL COLOUR ROUGH

The option eventually selected is a square design, broken by the tail, which includes vine motifs outside as well as inside the letter. The triangular silhouette of the four leaves placed around the O form of the Q makes up the corners of the square. The outside curves of the Q are angled, and the tail is given extra weight. Preliminary colour choices are made: gold for the letterform itself with mauve and green decoration.

1 *With the tracing paper firmly taped in position, an accurate pencil tracing is made of the outlines of the final design. After untaping the paper, the outlines are drawn on the reverse side of the paper in a soft pencil.*

2 *The design is transferred on to the chosen paper by placing the prepared tracing in position right side up. The outlines are drawn over again with a hard pencil so that the marks on the underside are transferred.*

3 *Gum ammoniac is applied to the letterform with a fine brush. The brush needs to be rinsed frequently in hot water to prevent the gum from clogging it. Breathing over the surface before the gold is applied restores tackiness.*

4 *Narrow strips of gold-transfer leaf are placed on the letterform, gold-side down. The backing sheet is removed after rubbing through it to adhere the gold to the gum ammoniac.*

5 *All parts of the letterform are covered in gold leaf, and the final piece of backing sheet is removed.*

6 *The gold is burnished with a burnishing tool through glassine paper. Tracing paper could be substituted. Afterward, any loose gold leaf is brushed away with a soft brush.*

7 *Sufficient quantities of the chosen colours of gouache are mixed to finish the job. The colour is carefully applied with a fine sable brush.*

8 *For the final version, it is decided to use a muted green for the decoration inside the counter.*

9 *The last elements to be completed are the fine tendrils that extend from the corners of the design.*

Gallery

The design and execution of illuminated letters brings together a variety of skills that the calligraphy beginner needs to develop. Not only are you concerned with the letterform itself, but also with the relationship of your illustration design to the letter and the work as a whole. Select colours carefully to enhance the balance between letterform and decoration. The examples on this page show a variety of approaches.

Wednesday, 25th October, 1826. Last night was one of the most dreadful I ever witnessed. The rain, driven by the violence of the wind, rendered it impossible for me to keep any fire, & to add misery to my affliction my tent was blown down at midnight, when I lay among pteris aquilina rolled in my wet blanket and tent till morning. Sleep of course was not to be had, every ten or fifteen minutes immense trees falling producing a crash as if the earth was cleaving asunder, which with

I LAY AMONG PTERIS AQUILINA — Mark Van Stone

In this rendering of a 19th-century text (above), medieval-style illumination has been used.

VERSAL CONCERTINA BOOK — Donald Jackson

These elegant compressed versals (above) show how a traditional letterform can be used in a contemporary context.

MEDIEVAL-STYLE ILLUMINATION — Mark Van Stone

This Latin text (left) is written and decorated in the style of the Lindisfarne Gospels. The watercolour decoration uses traditional Celtic knotwork motifs, and the following text is written in ink in insular half uncials.

Once you have mastered the basic letterforms, the scripts here and on the following pages will enable you to extend your calligraphic repertoire.

DOCEREM

it it befits the disciple t

ODIREDISC

RUSTICA

Rustic capitals were at their height of popularity from the fourth to sixth centuries A.D. for manuscript writing, but examples of the script dating from the second century have been found. In modern calligraphy, there are many uses for these stately letterforms.

Letter height: 7 nib widths.
Pen angle: 60°–90°. Some letters require twisting the pen.
O form: oval.
Slant: none.
Stroke number, order and direction: as annotated on alphabet.
Speed: slow.
Serifs: slightly curved slab-foot serifs.

Every scribe
instructed in
the kingdom
of heaven is like
a householder
who brings
forth out of
his treasury
new things

UNCIAL

This majuscule (capital) script was in widespread use from the third to the ninth centuries A.D. Its forms were influenced by both Greek and Roman precedents. The version illustrated here is known as angled-pen uncial and is more suited than some other forms to contemporary use.

Letter height: x height 3½ nib widths. Some letters extend above and below 2 nib widths more.
Pen angle: 20°.
O form: slightly extended circle.
Slant: none.
Stroke number, order and direction: as annotated on alphabet.
Speed: moderate.
Serifs: simple hooks.

over might

teeming w

home of sea

HALF UNCIAL

Dating from the sixth century A.D., this script was most beautifully written in the insular half uncials of England and Ireland.

Letter height: x height 3–4 nib widths, ascenders and descenders 1½–2 nib widths more.
Pen angle: 0°.
Slant: none.
Stroke number, order and direction: as annotated on alphabet.
Speed: moderately slow.
Serifs: club-shaped and built-up.

ABCDEFGHIIJ

KLMNOPQRST

UVWXYYZ

ABCDEEFGHIJKL

MNNOPQRSTTUV

VWXYYZ

abcdefghijk

lmnnopqrst

uvwxyz

CAROLINGIAN

The Carolingian minuscule is a flowing bookhand that developed during the late eighth century. It was accompanied by Roman versal or uncial capitals. It is a popular script for manuscript books.

Letter height: *x height 3 nib widths, ascenders and descenders 4 nib widths.*
Pen angle: *30°.*
O form: *slightly extended circle.*
Slant: *5°–10° to the right.*
Stroke number, order and direction: *as annotated on alphabet.*
Speed: *moderate.*
Serifs: *simple hooks.*

ou have grown so fast from the mould of the de

You have unfolded a hundred flowe

The hundred petalled golden flowers are fi

nd leaves are moist with the life giving water

OH SUN AND WATER AND GREEN GOLD

I WAS HERE AND NOW IN TH

ROTUNDA MINUSCULE

This rounded Gothic script of southern Europe was in use during the 13th to 15th centuries, and was particularly popular in Italy and Spain.

Letter height: *x height 4 nib widths, ascenders and descenders 2 nib widths more.*
Pen angle: *30°.*
O form: *squared-off circle.*
Slant: *none.*
Stroke number, order and direction: *as annotated on alphabet.*
Speed: *fairly slow.*
Serifs: *squared serifs for some stroke beginnings, and flattened endings to many vertical strokes, achieved by turning the nib to an angle of 0° at the bottom of a stroke.*

flowering sur

rich tapestr

stretching int

SHARPENED ITALIC

This angular form of italic dates from the 15th century. It was developed in Italy alongside the more rounded versions of the script. Like all italics, it may be joined or unjoined and can be plain (as shown here) or flourished.

Letter height: *x height 5 nib widths, ascenders and descenders 4 nib widths.*
Pen angle: *45°.*
O form: *sharpened oval.*
Slant: *5°–12° to the right.*
Stroke number, order and direction: *as annotated on alphabet.*
Speed: *moderate to fast.*
Serifs: *sharpened.*

abcddefghijkllm
nopqrstuvwxyyz

aabcdefffghhiijkl
mmmmnnopqrrsst
tuuuuvwxyyy3

abcdefghijklmno
pqrstuvwxyyz

Index

Credits

The publishers would like to thank all the calligraphers who submitted work for inclusion in the book and in particular the following who designed and produced the main projects in Part 5: **Lorraine Brady** (Letterhead); **John Neilson** (Poster and Manuscript book); **Timothy Noad** (Illuminated letter); **Penny Price** (Concertina book). The Invitation and Decorative border are by **Gaynor Goffe**. The Poetry broadsheet is by **Anna Ravenscroft**.

In addition, the publishers would like to thank the following: the Archer Press for printing the Letterhead; William Day (Engravers) Ltd for printing the Invitation; Hazel Bell for compiling the index; Karyn Gilman; David Kemp and Jane Royston for invaluable additional assistance.

Unless otherwise indicated, all calligraphic examples are by the authors.

Key: top (t); centre (c); below (b); left (l); right (r).

8 Anna Ronchi. 9 John Nash (t); The Board of Trinity College Dublin (l); Donald Jackson (b). 10 V & A Museum (t); Joan Pilsbury (b). 11 Reproduced by kind permission of Mrs Andrew Johnston. 12 Magnus Astrom. "Feuerharfe" by Yvan Goll from *Dichtungen*, ed. C. Goll (Hermann Luchterhand Verlag, 1960). © Yvan Goll. Reproduced by permission of Argon Verlag, Berlin (t); Florian Kynman. "The Shield of Achilles" from *Collected Poems* by W H Auden (Faber & Faber, 1991). © W H Auden. Reproduced by permission of Faber & Faber (UK), Random House (USA) (b). 13 Ewan Clayton. "Spring's Firebird" by Rumi from *Love's Fire* translated by Andrew Harvey (Jonathan Cape, 1988). © Andrew Harvey. Reproduced by permission of Random Century Group (UK), Aitken, Stone and Wylie (USA) (t); Julia Vance (b). 22 Gareth Colgan. 45 Teresa Dunstone (br). 52 Gareth Colgan. 53 Liz Burch. 54 British Library. 55 Joan Pilsbury. 64 Angela Swann. 65 Claire Secrett. 76 John Neilson. 78 Bodleian Library, Oxford (t); Joan Pilsbury (b). 83 Gareth Colgan. 92 Louise Donaldson. 93 Liz Burch. 104 Paivi Vesanto. 105 Julia Vance. From *North* by Seamus Heaney (Faber & Faber, 1978). © Seamus Heaney. Reproduced by permission of Faber & Faber (UK) and Farrar, Strauss & Giroux (USA). 108 Paivi Vesanto. 112 Lawrence R. Brady. 114 Bodleian Library, Oxford 122–123 Anna Ravenscroft. 129 Anna Ravenscroft. 131 Anna Ravenscroft. 137 Angela Hickey (t); Timothy Noad (l); Bonnie Leah (br). 141 Bonnie Leah (t); Christopher Haanes (tr); Georgia Deaver (l); Elizabeth Rounce (bl). 145 Louise Donaldson (l); Janet Mehigan (r). 146 Nancy R. Leavitt (tl); Julia Vance (b); Paivi Vesanto (r). 147 Sheila Waters. "Tor House" from *The Selected Poetry of Robinson Jeffers* (Random House, 1959) © Robinson Jeffers. Reproduced by permission of W. W. Norton & Co (t); Gillian Hazeldine. From the *Exter Riddle Book* translated by Kevin Crossley-Holland (The Folio Society, 1978). © Kevin Crossley-Holland. Reproduced by permission of The Folio Society and Kevin Crossley-Holland. 151 Jenny Kavarana (l & b); Louise Donaldson (t). 155 Mary Noble (t); Anne Irwin; Patricia Lovett (b). 156–161 From *Strong Tea* by John B. Keane. Reproduced by permission of The Mercier Press, Cork. 160 Hazel Dolby (t); Kate Ridyard. From *Selected Poems* translated by Anthony Kerrigan (Jonathan Cape, 1970). Reproduced by permission of Random Century Group (b). 161 Monica Dengo (t); Suzanne Moore (l); Joan Pilsbury (r). 165 Carina Westling (t); Joan Pilsbury and Wendy Westover (l); Gaynor Goffe (r). 169 Mark Van Stone (t & l); Donald Jackson (r). 170 Gareth Colgan. 171 Gareth Colgan (t); Lorraine Brady (b). 172 Louise Donaldson (t); Kate Ridyard (b).